THIRD EDITION

Well Said

Pronunciation for Clear Communication

LINDA GRANT

HEINLE
CENGAGE Learning

Australia • Brazil • Japan • Korea • Mexico • Singapore • Spain • United Kingdom • United States

HEINLE
CENGAGE Learning

Well Said:
Pronunciation for Clear Communication,
Third Edition
Linda Grant

Publisher: Sherrise Roehr

Acquisition Editor: Tom Jefferies

Assistant Development Editor: Marissa Petrarca

Assistant Development Editor: Cécile Engeln

Director of Content and Media Production:
  Michael Burggren

Marketing Director, U.S.: Jim McDonough

Senior Product Marketing Manager:
  Caitlin Driscol

Senior Content Project Manager:
  Maryellen Eschmann-Killeen

Print Buyer: Susan Carrol

Cover Design: Lori Stuart

Composition: PrePress PMG

For product information and technology assistance, contact us at
Cengage Learning Customer & Sales Support, 1-800-354-9706

For permission to use material from this text or product,
submit all requests online at **cengage.com/permissions**
Further permissions questions can be e-mailed to
permissionrequest@cengage.com.

Library of Congress Control Number: 2008943256
ISBN 10: 1-4240-0625-2
ISBN 13: 978-1-4240-0625-0

Heinle
20 Channel Center Street
Boston, MA 02210
USA

Cengage Learning is a leading provider of customized learning solutions with office locations around the globe, including Singapore, the United Kingdom, Australia, Mexico, Brazil, and Japan. Locate your local office at: **international.cengage.com/region**

Cengage Learning products are represented in Canada by Nelson Education, Ltd.

Visit Heinle online at **elt.heinle.com**
Visit our corporate website at **cengage.com**

Printed in United States of America
3 4 5 6 7   11

Contents

To the Instructor vi

New Features of the Third Edition vii

To the Student ix

Part I: Introductory Chapters

1 **Your Pronunciation Profile** 1
  The Speech Profile 1
  Speech Profile Form 4
  Needs and Attitudes Assessment 5
  Setting Personal Goals 7

2 **Using a Dictionary for Pronunciation** 9
  Introduction to Dictionary Symbols 9
  Pronunciation Guide for *Well Said, Third Edition* 16

Part II: Getting Started with Sounds and Syllables

3 **Consonant Sounds and Spellings** 19
  Listen! 20
  Rules and Practices 1: Unusual Consonant Spelling Patterns 21
  Rules and Practices 2: Final Consonant Sounds and Spellings 28
  Communicative Practice: Evacuate! 33
  Oral Review—Sound and Spelling Patterns 36

4 **Syllables and Word Endings** 37
  Listen! 37
  Rules and Practices 1: Syllables and –*s* Endings 39
  Rules and Practices 2: Syllables and –*ed* Endings 45
  Communicative Practice: Two Truths and a "Tale" 47
  TOEFL® iBT Speaking Practice 49
  Extend Your Skills . . . to Descriptions of Graphs 50
  Explaining a Graph/Self- or Peer-Evaluation Form 51
  Oral Review—Syllables and Word Endings 54

Part III: Stress, Rhythm, and Intonation

5 **Stress in Words** 55
  Listen! 55
  Rules and Practices: Using Parts of Speech to Predict Stress 57
  Communicative Practice: No E-mail Fridays 67

6 **Stress in Longer Words** **69**
Listen! 70
Rules and Practices: Using Suffixes to Predict Stress 72
Communicative Practice: Library Orientation 77
Extend Your Skills . . . to a Small-Group Discussion 79
Oral Review—Stress in Words 82
Beyond the Pronunciation Classroom: Applying for a Library Card 83
Midcourse Self-Evaluation 84

7 **Rhythm in Phrases and Sentences** **85**
Listen! 86
Rules and Practices: Stressed and Reduced Words 90
Communicative Practice: Scheduling an Appointment 100
Extend Your Skills . . . to Recording a Message 101
Oral Review: Rhythm in Phrases and Sentences 102
Beyond the Pronunciation Classroom: Knock! Knock! Jokes 102

8 **Thought Groups and Focus Words** **103**
Listen! 103
Rules and Practices 1: Thought Groups 106
Rules and Practices 2: Normal or Basic Focus Words 108
Rules and Practices 3: Special or Marked Focus Words 110
TOEFL iBT® Speaking Practice 119
Communicative Practice: Announcing Schedule Changes 120
Oral Review—Thought Groups and Focus Words 121
Beyond the Pronunciation Classroom: Comparing Business Practices 122

9 **Intonation: Falling and Rising Tones** **123**
Listen! 123
Rules and Practices 1: Intonation at the End of Sentences 125
Rules and Practices 2: Intonation at the End of Non-Final Thought Groups . . 134
TOEFL iBT® Speaking Practice 136
Communicative Practice: Interviews and Surveys 139
Oral Review: Final Intonation—Falling and Rising Tones 140
Beyond the Pronunciation Classroom: Placing a Food Order 140

10 **Linking and Connected Speech** **141**
Listen! 142
Rules and Practices 1: Linking and Sound Change 142
Communicative Practice: Driving Test 148
Extend Your Skills . . . to a Process Presentation 149
Process Presentation/Self-Evaluation Form 150
Oral Review—Putting It All Together 151
Beyond the Pronunciation Classroom: Checking Air Fares 153

Part IV: Consonants and Vowels

CS

Consonant Supplements

Supplement 1:   The Phonetic Alphabet   155

Supplement 2:   Voiceless and Voiced Sounds
                /p/ *p*ie – /b/ *b*uy
                /t/ *t*ime – /d/ *d*ime
                /k/ ba*ck* – /g/ ba*g* 156

Supplement 3:   Continuants and Stops
                /s/ *ni*ce – /t/ nigh*t* 159

Supplement 4:   The Speech Pathway and the Consonant Chart 160

Supplement 5:   /θ/ *th*in – /s/ *s*in
                /θ/ *th*in – /t/ *t*in
                /θ/ *th*in – /f/ *f*in 162

Supplement 6:   /f/ *f*air – /p/ *p*air 166

Supplement 7:   /ʃ/ *sh*eet – /s/ *s*eat
                /ʃ/ *sh*eet – /tʃ/ *ch*eat 170

Supplement 8:   /r/ *r*ight – /l/ *l*ight
                /r/ g*r*ad – /l/ g*l*ad 174

Supplement 9:   /v/ *v*ery – /w/ *w*ary
                /v/ *v*ery – /b/ *b*erry 180

VS

Vowel Supplements

Supplement 10: Front, Central, Back Vowels, and Diphthongs 185

Supplement 11: Phonetic Alphabet and Vowel Chart 187

Supplement 12: Tense and Lax Vowels 188

Supplement 13: /ɪ/ *f*i*t*   – /iʸ/ in *fee*t 189

Supplement 14: /ɛ/ *pen*   – /eʸ/ *pain*
                /ɛ/ *pen*   – /æ/ *pan* 193

Supplement 15: /ʌ/ *l*u*ck*   – /ɑ/ in *lock* 196

Supplement 16: /ɜr/ *girl*   – /ʌ/ *gull* 200

Supplement 17: /oʷ/*note*   – /ɑ/ *not* 201

Info Gap Activities 207

Appendix A: Strategies for Independent Learning 213

Appendix B: Noun-Verb Pairs 217

Appendix C: Guidelines for Word Stress 219

Appendix D: Guidelines for Focus Words 223

Answer Key: Selected Exercises Chapters 1–10 225

Answer Key: Consonant Supplements 226

Answer Key: Vowel Supplements 231

Skills Index 235

CD Index 239

To the Instructor

Welcome to the third edition of *Well Said*. This text and audio program aims to improve the pronunciation of high-intermediate to advanced students so they can communicate with clarity and confidence. For beginning to intermediate students, see *Well Said Intro,* a lower-level text in the *Well Said* series.

Well Said, Third Edition, was written for general English learners but is especially useful for students in academic, business, scientific, and professional settings. The text is flexible and can be used in classrooms, labs, small groups, tutorials, and for self-study.

Well Said, Third Edition, meets the pronunciation needs of students from many language backgrounds. The body of the text focuses on the music of the language — syllables, stress, rhythm, thought groups, and intonation — features that can be problematic for students from most language backgrounds. The learning supplements provide individualized practice for selected consonant and vowel sounds. These problems vary among students.

Well Said was written to respond to challenges the pronunciation teacher faces in today's classroom:

- Individualizing pronunciation teaching to meet the needs of diverse groups of learners
- Guiding learners into natural, relevant communicative contexts so that transfer of pronunciation into speaking is not left entirely to chance
- Establishing reasonable measures of progress that account for different rates of acquisition and for the role of the learner in evaluation and monitoring
- Providing a course that links pronunciation with listening and speaking so that teachers do not have to supplement with materials from other skill areas.

In addition, *Well Said, Third Edition*, offers these helpful strategies and features:

- An introductory chapter that identifies needs and priorities for individual students and the class
- Emphasis on stress, rhythm, and intonation to improve overall intelligibility
- Consonant- and vowel-learning supplements that provide an overview of all consonants and vowels as well as intensive practice with sounds that are difficult for most students
- Multi-sensory practice that helps students internalize new skills
- Progression from controlled practice into natural communicative contexts
- "Prime-Time Practice" for homework in pronunciation, listening, and self-monitoring
- "Beyond the Pronunciation Classroom" to prepare students for real-world interactions with proficient English speakers
- Activities that maximize student talking time and provide enough practice to enable students to assimilate elements of clear speech into oral communication.

New Features of the Third Edition

- Chapter reorganization that introduces thought groups earlier in the text
- Strategies and exercises that reflect the latest research in pronunciation
- Vocabulary choices, phrasal contexts, and high-frequency stress patterns informed by corpus linguistics. Sources include the Academic Word List (Coxhead), MICASE, Cobuild Concordance and Collocations Sampler, and research on common stress patterns in academic words
- "You Choose!" segments that integrate consonant and vowel practice with stress, rhythm, and intonation
- Authentic speech samples that provide models of proficient native and non-native English speakers
- New TOEFL exercises that link pronunciation practice to specific Speaking Tasks on the TOEFL® iBT
- Audio CDs indexed to each exercise

Organization of the Text

The organization of the text is based on pronunciation features. Syllables, stress, and intonation are the focus of Chapter 1 through 10. Consonants and vowels are the focus of Supplements 1 through 17.

Moving in sequence through the chapters will result in a coherent presentation. Instructors, however, can establish their own priorities and set alternate paths through the material. Considerations for reorganizing chapters are included in the *Instructor's Manual*.

Chapter 1 contains a diagnostic instrument and tools for learner self-evaluation and goal setting. These instruments motivate students, provide individual and class profiles, and suggest which parts of the book to emphasize. Chapter 2 explores the dictionary for pronunciation purposes and introduces pronunciation features covered in later chapters. Chapters 3 through 10 cover the high-priority stress, rhythm, and intonation features. While working through the chapters, instructors can integrate selected consonant and vowel supplements as needed, desired, or suggested by "You Choose" boxes.

Organization Within Chapters

Except for the first two introductory chapters, all chapters follow a similar progression. Each chapter begins with a "Listen!" segment to help students perceive the target feature in each chapter and build skills for peer and self-monitoring.

In the next section, "Rules and Practices," students discover pronunciation rules and guidelines. The practices and exercises help students gain control of pronunciation features before applying them in more challenging communicative contexts.

In "Communicative Practice," learners incorporate pronunciation concepts into contextualized speaking activities that naturally elicit numerous instances of the teaching point. These activities guide learners as they bridge the gap between a focus on accuracy and a focus on meaning. It is important that students not be expected to use features 100 percent correctly, or even 50 percent correctly, in these activities. Rather, they can use these opportunities to test hypotheses, make mistakes, correct mistakes, and observe how pronunciation concepts affect meaning in communication.

"Extend Your Skills . . ." recycles target pronunciation features into typical academic, business, and workplace speaking formats (graph explanation, problem solving, discussion, contrastive analysis, and process presentation). This section includes suggestions for recording and self-evaluating pronunciation.

"Prime-Time Practice" assigns homework for out-of-class practice. These lessons sometimes include self-monitoring and teacher feedback. Most chapters end with an "Oral Review," which students can complete either as a final review or as an end-of-chapter quiz.

As students become more comfortable with new pronunciation patterns, Chapters 6 through 10 conclude with "Beyond the Pronunciation Classroom." This segment helps students rehearse for and then transfer pronunciation awareness into real-world interactions.

Tips, incentives, and strategies for pronunciation practice called "Something to Think About" and "A Helpful Hint" are seeded throughout all of the chapters.

The Supplements contain an overview of all consonants and vowels, as well as intensive pronunciation practice with selected sounds. The Supplements also contain listening and speaking exercises for individuals and small groups and "Communicative Practice" for in- or out-of-class small-group work. The Answer Keys for supplements are at the end of the student text.

In general, the text encourages the learner to be actively involved in the process of becoming a clear speaker of English and to view the instructor as a guide or coach.

Instructor's Manual

The *Instructor's Manual* provides novice and experienced pronunciation instructors with teaching suggestions, theoretical underpinnings, rationale for activities, and additional exercises. It also includes answer keys, audio scripts, and references.

Audio Program

The audio program enables students to obtain additional out-of-class practice or to work through the text independently. Instructors can use the audio in the classroom at their discretion. Teachers who do not use the audio will find transcripts in the *Instructor's Manual*.

Progress in Pronunciation Improvement

Although more research is needed in learning pronunciation in a second or foreign language, here are characteristics you may notice:

- Individuals vary in the rate and extent of pronunciation improvement. Progress is influenced by such factors as motivation, personality, the first language, and amount of conversation outside of class.

- New pronunciation skills are acquired over time. At the beginning, using new sounds requires conscious attention. With time and practice, skills become more automatic. New skills often occur in controlled speaking or reading activities before they are evident in spontaneous speech. New skills may be most difficult to incorporate when the speaking demands are heavy.

- Errors are an expected and natural part of the learning process. Learners might approximate features before they can produce them clearly. They may overgeneralize patterns before refining them. They may lose former skills while acquiring new ones. In short, teachers cannot measure learning based simply on a student's accurate oral productions.

- Learners might only partially integrate new pronunciation features into spontaneous speech. However, even partial integration of a new pronunciation skill has a positive overall effect on intelligibility.

As our knowledge of pronunciation in a second language grows, I hope this text serves as an effective guide for improving pronunciation in everyday communication. I appreciate hearing from users of *Well Said*. If you have suggestions, comments or questions, please forward them to me through the publisher.

Linda Grant

To the Student

Many of you can read, write, and understand American English well, but your pronunciation may interfere with clear and effective communication. This text/audio program will help you improve your pronunciation so that you can communicate confidently and be understood with ease.

In this course, you will focus on common pronunciation problems for high-intermediate to advanced learners of English. You will practice pronunciation in structured exercises and less structured real-life communication activities. As you progress through the text, your pronunciation of new patterns gradually will require less conscious attention and become more automatic.

You will work individually and with partners, small groups, and the whole class. You will practice both speaking and listening to English. As a listener, you will hear examples of clear and unclear pronunciation from class members. This is not wasted time. This listening practice will help you learn what makes speech clear and easy to understand. It will also help you monitor and correct your *own* pronunciation.

Here are a few more points to consider as you begin:

- Mistakes are a natural and necessary part of learning, so don't be afraid to make them.

- You won't eliminate your accent or speak with 100 percent accuracy. A more realistic goal is to change the aspects of your pronunciation that interfere with your being understood clearly. You do not need to sound like a native speaker of English to be fully and easily understood.

- Your attitude is important in pronunciation improvement. You will make more progress if you are strongly motivated to improve.
- You will incorporate the concepts presented in this text more quickly if you listen to and speak English outside of the classroom.

I hope *Well Said, Third Edition,* helps you in your efforts to become a clear speaker of English.

ACKNOWLEDGMENTS

Thanks to writers/researchers/colleagues who have prodded my thinking about second language speech-pronunciation-listening. They include Bill Acton, Richard Cauldwell, Tracey Derwing, John Field, Judy Gilbert, Janet Goodwin, John Levis, David Mendelsohn, Colleen Meyers, Sue Miller, Joan Morley, Murray Munro, Lucy Pickering, Ann Wennerstrom, and Rita Wong.

These reviewers of the third edition deserve special thanks: Cathleen Jacobson, Jamie Kirchner, John Levis, and Karen Tucker.

Special thanks also to my editors at Heinle, Cengage Learning, especially to Thomas Jefferies, Marissa Petrarca, Tunde Dewey, and Maryellen Killeen (for guiding yet another edition through production with expertise and encouragement); and, last but not least, to Jim, for infinite patience.

Credits

Page 4, Speech Profile Form: The scale was adapted from (1) American Council on the Teaching of Foreign Languages (ACTFL), Proficiency Guidelines (Hastings-on-Hudson, N.Y.: ACTFL, 1986), by permission of ACTFL. See below for a complete list of references; and from (2) Joan Morley, "EFL/ESL Intelligibility Index," How Many Languages Do You Speak? Nagoya Gakuin Daigaku: Gaikokugo Kyoiku Kiyo No. 19, Jan./Feb. 1988.

ACTFL REFERENCES

American Council on the Teaching of Foreign Languages. Proficiency Guidelines. Hastings-on-Hudson, N.Y.: ACTFL, 1986.

Draper, Jamie B. State Initiatives and Activities in Foreign Languages and International Studies. Monograph. Washington, D.C.: Joint National Committee for Languages, 1986.

_____. The State of the States: State Initiatives in Foreign Languages and International Studies. Monograph. Washington, D.C.: Joint National Committee for Languages, 1989.

Eddy, Peter A. "The Effect of Foreign Language Study in High School on Verbal Ability as Measured by the Scholastic Aptitude Test—Verbal." Washington, D.C.: Center for Applied Linguistics, 1981.

Masciantonio, Rudolph. "Tangible Benefits of the Study of Latin: A Review of Research." Foreign Language Annals 10 (1977): 376–377.

National Council of State Supervisors of Foreign Languages. Distance Learning in Foreign Languages: A Position Paper with Guidelines. Monograph. Washington, D.C.: National Council of State Supervisors of Foreign Languages, 1990.

New York State Board of Regents. New York State Board of Regents Action Plan to Improve Elementary and Secondary Education Results. Albany, N.Y.: University of the State of New York, State Education Department, 1984.

Panetta, Leon. "The Quiet Crisis of Global Competence." Northeast Conference Newsletter 30 (Fall 1991): 14–17.

Page 9, Cartoon: © The New Yorker Collection 1972 Mischa Richter from cartoonbank.com. All Rights Reserved. **Page 19, Cartoon:** © The New Yorker Collection 1991 Leo Cullum from cartoonbank.com. All Rights Reserved. **Page 33, Evacuate:** Adapted from Connie L. Shoemaker and F. Floyd Shoemaker, Interactive techniques for the ESL Classroom (New York: Newbury House Publishers, 1991), p. 128–129. Used with permission. **Page 38, Color Preference:** Information Adapted from "The Blueing of America," Time, July 18, 1983, p 62; Leslie Kane, "The Power of Color," Health, July 1982, p 37; Faber Birren, *Color and Human Response*, John Wiley and Sons, 1984; Chattapadhyay, Amitvava: Gorn, Gerald & Darker, Peter (2000). East, west, blue is best. http://www.bm.ust.hk/newsletter/autumn2000/autumn00-10.html **Page 40, Cartoon:** © The New Yorker Collection 1998 J.P. Rini from cartoonbank.com. All rights Reserved. **Page 50, Cartoon:** © The New Yorker

Your Pronunciation Profile

A *pronunciation profile* is a general description of your pronunciation abilities and needs. It is not a test. The profile alerts you and your teacher to the parts of this book that will be of most help to you and to the class.

The speaking activities in the first part of this chapter form the basis of your profile. The pronunciation profile has three parts:

Part A: Reading a Paragraph

Part B: Answering Interview Questions

Part C: Introducing a Partner

Do as many of the speaking activities as you can. The more speaking you do, the better your teacher will be able to identify your pronunciation strengths and weaknesses.

During the speaking activities, your teacher can record observations about your pronunciation on the *Speech Profile Form* on page 4. At the end of this course, you can repeat **Part A:** Reading a Paragraph to assess improvement.

The Speech Profile

Part A: Reading a Paragraph

Choose only one of the paragraphs below. Read it silently for meaning. Then read it out loud as naturally as possible. You can either schedule an individual consultation with your teacher or submit a recording.

READING 1

Have you ever watched young children practice the sounds of the language they are learning? They imitate, repeat, and sing consonant and vowel combinations without effort. For young children, learning to speak a language is natural and automatic. No one would suspect that complex learning is occurring. For adult learners, however, pronunciation of a new language is not automatic. It presents an unusual challenge.

Why is pronunciation progress in adults more limited? Some researchers say the reasons are biological or physical. Others say they are social or cultural. Although many questions are still unanswered, it's important to realize two things about clear speaking. First, pronunciation improvement might be a challenge, but almost everyone makes progress. Second, adults can learn to communicate clearly in English without giving up their accents or their identification with their native cultures.

READING 2

Why do some students make more pronunciation progress than others? Do they just have a special talent for language learning? Natural ability is important, but there are other factors too. One factor is the mother tongue. In general, it takes less time to learn the pronunciation of a language that is similar to one's own. Another key factor is motivation. If students have a strong need to speak English clearly, they will usually make more progress. Closely related to motivation is attitude. Students who identify with a culture are more willing to sound like the speakers from that culture. A fourth factor is practice outside of the classroom. Students who have conversations with English speakers in everyday situations improve their pronunciation more quickly. Based on these points, what can students do to facilitate their own progress?

Part B: Answering Interview Questions

Record short responses to each item. You may make brief notes, but do not write or rehearse your answers.

1. Talk briefly about your family. (30–45 seconds)

2. Describe your school or work background and your purpose for studying English. (30–45 seconds)

3. Describe your most pleasant childhood memory. (30–45 seconds)

Part C: Introducing a Partner

In class, interview a person whom you do not know well. Take brief notes. Choose the most interesting pieces of information and introduce your partner to the class.

Name: _____

Birth country _____

First language _____

First job _____

Favorite movie _____

Biggest challenge _____

Best advice _____

A perfect day _____

Ambition _____

Other: _____ _____

_____

Speech Profile Form*

Name: _____ Date: _____

     The activities in Chapter 1 indicate that you need to concentrate on these pronunciation features.

Features of Speech	Specific Difficulties	Examples
Consonants (Chapter 3; Supplements 1–9)		
Vowels (Supplements 10–17)		
Grammatical Endings (Chapter 4)		
Stress in Words (Chapters 5 and 6)		
General Rhythm (Chapter 7)		
Thought Groups (Chapters 8 and 9)		
Focus (Chapters 8 and 9)		
Final and Non-Final Intonation Patterns (Chapter 9)		
Linking and Connected Speech (Chapter 10)		
Delivery (rate of speech, loudness, eye contact, posture, movement, and gestures):		

THREE PRONUNCIATION STRENGTHS:

    1. _____

    2. _____

    3. _____

THREE PRONUNCIATION PRIORITIES:

    1. _____

    2. _____

    3. _____

*To be completed by the instructor. See the *Instructor Manual* for a more detailed *Speech Profile Form.*

Something to Think About

Maybe you are having trouble with some **consonant and vowel sounds.** Or maybe you are not sure how English **stress, rhythm, and intonation work.** Both areas affect how well you are understood. But if you have limited time to work on pronunciation, focus on your priorities—pronunciation points that will improve your speech the most.

A priority might be an error that is frequent. Or it might be a feature that has a greater effect on overall intelligibility. For most students, **stress, rhythm, and intonation** improve overall intelligibility more than sounds. Why? Sounds usually affect a listener's understanding of words. But stress, rhythm, and intonation affect a listener's understanding of phrases, sentences, and even conversations!

Needs and Attitudes Assessment

This tool helps your teacher plan a course for your needs. Circle the answers, and then discuss your answers with a small group or your class.

A. Speaking Skills	Ability (1 = good 2 = average 3 = weak)
1. Using appropriate nonverbal communication (eye contact, gestures, etc.)	1 . . . 2 . . . 3
2. Speaking confidently	1 . . . 2 . . . 3
3. Speaking at a good speed	1 . . . 2 . . . 3
4. Speaking at a good volume	1 . . . 2 . . . 3
5. Understanding casual speech	1 . . . 2 . . . 3

B. Speaking Tasks	Importance (1 = not 2 = somewhat 3 = very)	Ability (1 = good 2 = average 3 = weak)
1. Participating in informal conversations	1...2...3	1...2...3
2. Participating in discussions/meetings	1...2...3	1...2...3
3. Giving presentations	1...2...3	1...2...3
4. Giving explanations or instructions	1...2...3	1...2...3
5. Talking on the phone	1...2...3	1...2...3
6. Other:	1...2...3	1...2...3

What is your easiest speaking situation?

What is your most difficult speaking situation?

Which listeners do you especially want to understand you?

C. Pronunciation Skills	Example	Ability
1. Using English word stress	e $\overline{CO}$ no my e co $\overline{NO}$ mi cal	1...2...3
2. Stressing more important words; reducing less important words	The QUIZ is on TUESday.	1...2...3
3. Dividing speech into logical phrases or thought groups	The QUIZ on TUESday / was MOVED to FRIday.	1...2...3
4. Emphasizing the key word in each thought group	The QUIZ on **TUES**day / was MOVED to **FRI**day.	1...2...3
5. Using appropriate final intonation	It's on **FRI**day? ↗ (uncertainty) It's on **FRI**day. ↘ (certainty)	1...2...3
6. Using clear word endings	They (ser<u>ve</u>, ser<u>ve</u>d) in the military.	1...2...3

7. Using clear consonants	(Col<u>l</u>ect/Co<u>rr</u>ect) the papers.	1...2...3
8. Using clear vowels in stressed syllables and reduced vowels in unstressed syllables	/ɛ/ /ə/ ME - thod	1...2...3

In what two or three pronunciation areas do you most want to improve?

D. Attitudes

1. What sounds and patterns of English pronunciation do you like (e.g., what do you like the sound of; what do you like saying)?

2. What sounds and patterns of English pronunciation do you dislike (e.g., what do you dislike the sound of; what do you dislike saying)?

3. What English speaker do you admire? Why?

Setting Personal Goals

How intelligible or clear is your speech? How intelligible do you need or want to be? Use the scale on page 8 to judge your intelligibility. Put a check (✔) on the scale to indicate your pronunciation proficiency *now*. Put an asterisk (*) on the scale to indicate your *goal*.

Something to Think About

When setting goals, be realistic. For most adults, it is not realistic to aim for a native-like pronunciation (position 6 or beyond on the scale). Why?

- **It may not be possible.** Most adult students do not eliminate all traces of their accent.

- **It is not necessary.** You can speak English clearly and be fully understood, yet keep aspects of your accent.

- **It may not be desirable.** Your accent is important because it identifies you with your native language and culture.

There are many standards and varieties of English. Most speakers on the audio program use general North American English, but you will hear some speakers of other dialects and varieties as well.

Pronunciation Proficiency Scale

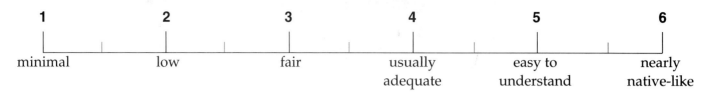

1	2	3	4	5	6
minimal	low	fair	usually adequate	easy to understand	nearly native-like

1 **Minimal:** Listener understands only occasional words

2 **Low:** Very difficult for listener to understand, even one accustomed to speaking with nonnative speakers; listener needs constant repetition

3 **Fair:** Somewhat intelligible to native speakers who are accustomed to speaking with nonnative speakers; frequent pronunciation variations interfere on two levels—they cause misunderstanding *and* distract the listener

4 **Usually Adequate:** Intelligible to most native speakers; accent and pronunciation variations only occasionally cause misunderstanding but are still distracting; listener has to make effort to overcome the distraction

5 **Easy to understand:** Obvious accent; patterned pronunciation variations, but they neither cause misunderstanding nor distract the listener; listener can attend to the content of the message

6 **Nearly native-like:** Rare, isolated mispronunciations with no patterns of error; barely detectable accent; pronunciation is almost like that of native speakers

Keep the results of this scale. Refer back midway through the course to reassess your goals.

Using a Dictionary for Pronunciation

Introduction to Dictionary Symbols

You can use your dictionary for more than just word definitions. Your dictionary is also a useful pronunciation resource, especially when you can anticipate the vocabulary you will need for a discussion or presentation.

Dictionaries use special symbols for pronunciation, but the symbols can be confusing because they vary from dictionary to dictionary. Standard English dictionaries usually use symbols like those in the cartoon above. Dictionaries for English students, however, usually use a version of the International Phonetic Alphabet (IPA). This chapter will help you understand the symbols in *your* dictionary, whether you use a standard English dictionary or a dictionary for students learning English, such as the *Collins COBUILD Dictionary of American English* or *The Newbury House Dictionary of American English (NHD)*.

1 **Syllables:** Each vowel sound in a word creates a beat or syllable. For example, *present* has two vowel sounds and two beats. Some dictionaries separate syllables with dots.

> pre•sent
>
> pre•si•dent

Syllables for *writing* are often indicated in the first entry word; syllables for *speaking* are often indicated in parentheses or between slanted lines.

> pre•sent   /prɛ zənt/
>
> pre•si•dent   /prɛ zə dənt/

The number of written syllables and the number of spoken syllables are occasionally different:

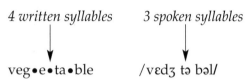

4 written syllables   *3 spoken syllables*

> veg•e•ta•ble   /vɛdʒ tə bəl/

Exercise 1

Guess how many spoken syllables are in each word below. Then check your dictionary. Write each word in the correct column.

arrive	please	immediate	cereal
text	authority	page	video
manager	dictionary	business	chocolate

1 syllable	**2 syllables**	**3 syllables**	**4 syllables**
own	jun•ior	po•si•tive	com•pe•ti•tion
_____	_____	_____	_____
_____	_____	_____	_____
_____	_____	_____	_____

CD 1; Track 1 Say the words in each column with your teacher or the speaker on audio. How does *your* dictionary show number of syllables? _____

2 **Stress:** All dictionaries show primary stress, the strongest syllable in a word. Some underline the vowel in the stressed syllable. Others use a boldface mark before /'/ or after (´) the syllable with primary stress.

> pre•si•dent   /'prɛ zə dənt/   *From a learner dictionary*
>
> pre•si•dent   (prĕz´ĭ-dənt)   *From a standard English dictionary*

Exercise 2

Guess where the primary stress is in each word. Then mark the primary stress, according to *your* dictionary. The first one has been done for you.

1. ca 'nal

2. tech no lo gy

3. tech no lo gi cal

4. ap pre ci ate

5. hy po the sis

6. pro duce (noun)

7. pro duce (verb)

8. mi no ri ty

How does *your* dictionary mark primary stress? _____

CD 1; Track 2 Say the words with your teacher or the speaker on audio.

3 **Vowels with Name Sounds:** Vowels with name sounds, sometimes called *long* vowels, are pronounced like their letter names.

A Helpful Hint

When a one-syllable word has two vowel letters, the first vowel usually says its *name*, and the second vowel is silent.

In *paid*,	*a* says its name, A,	and *i* is silent.
In *cheat*,	*e* says its name, E,	and *a* is silent.
In *ride*,	*i* says its name, I,	and *e* is silent.
In *road*,	*o* says its name, O,	and *a* is silent.
In *use*,	*u* says its name, ∪,	and *e* is silent.

In elementary schools in the United States, children are sometimes taught this rhyme: "When two vowels go walking, the first one does the talking."

To represent name sounds, most dictionaries for English learners use IPA symbols. Standard dictionaries use this symbol (–) over the vowels.

paid /peɪd/   *From a learner dictionary*

paid (pād)   *From a standard English dictionary*

Exercise 3

Write the vowel symbol *your* dictionary uses for vowels in italics. Then find the key word for each symbol in the Pronunciation Guide in *your* dictionary. The first one has been done for you using a *learner dictionary*.

LETTER NAME	WORDS	SYMBOL	KEY WORD
1. A	f*a*ce and p*ai*nt	eɪ	name
2. E	s*ea*t and m*ee*t		
3. I	h*i*ke and m*igh*t		
4. O	r*o*le and go*a*l		
5. U	*u*se and d*ue*		

CD 1; Track 3 Repeat the words after your teacher or the speaker on audio.

4 **Vowels with Base Sounds:** Vowels with base sounds are sometimes called *short vowels.* In one-syllable words, base sounds are usually single vowel letters. They are *often* preceded by a consonant and *always* followed by a consonant (e.g., *plan, met, if, cost, but*).

To represent base sounds, most dictionaries for English learners use IPA symbols. Standard dictionaries use this symbol (˘) or no mark over the vowel.

plan /plæn/ *From a learner dictionary*

plan (plăn) *From a standard English dictionary* Backards ε

Exercise 4

feather

Write the symbols *your* dictionary uses for the vowels in italics. Then find the key word for each symbol in your dictionary's Pronunciation Guide. The first item has been done for you using a *learner dictionary*.

WORDS	SYMBOL	KEY WORD
1. t*a*x and p*a*ck	æ	cat
2. y*e*s and Fr*e*nch		
3. pr*i*nt and b*ui*lding	ε	
4. h*o*t and c*o*py	A	
5. r*u*sh and w*o*n	ΙΛΙ	

CD 1; Track 4 Say the words after your teacher or the speaker on audio.

5 **The Schwa Vowel Sound:** Vowels in stressed syllables are clear, but vowels in unstressed syllables tend to be unclear. Unstressed syllables often contain the neutral sound of schwa /ə/, as in **a**bout or **u**s. For that reason, schwa is the most common vowel sound in North American English. Most dictionaries use the symbol /ə/ for the schwa.

> a•vail•a•ble /ə'veɪ lə bəl/   *From a learner dictionary*
>
> a•vail•a•ble (ə-vā′lə -bəl)   *From a standard English dictionary*

Exercise 5

With a partner, guess where the schwa /ə/ occurs in these words. Then look the words up in a dictionary. Underline the schwa sounds.

1. mi nor   **3.** com mon   **5.** ac a dem ic

2. mi nor i ty   **4.** com pete   **6.** pro tec tion

CD 1; Track 5   Repeat the words after your teacher or the speaker on audio.

6 **Consonant Sounds:** English consonants are not always pronounced the way they are spelled.

Exercise 6

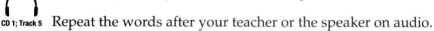

homonyms => their => there => they're

Write the symbol your dictionary uses for the italicized letters in each set of words. Then find the key word for each symbol in your dictionary's Pronunciation Guide. The first one was done using a *learner dictionary*.

-loose => tight

		SYMBOL	KEY WORD
1. *z*ero lose clo*s*e *(verb)* ra*z*or		/z/	ZOO
2. *sh*ow ini*ti*ate pre*ss*ure spe*c*ial			
3. *ch*eck furni*t*ure na*t*ure si*t*uation			
4. divi*s*ion u*s*ually A*s*ia bei*g*e			
5. *j*oke gra*d*uate a*g*ent sche*d*ule			
6. ma*x*imum e*x*treme e*x*plain a*cc*ept			

CD 1; Track 6   Repeat the words after your teacher or the speaker on audio.

A Helpful Hint

You can improve your intelligibility in a discussion or presentation if you correct the pronunciation of one or two key terms that are likely to occur over and over. Develop the habit of predicting key words that you will need for meetings or discussions. Make sure you can pronounce the words. Look them up or ask a proficient English speaker to say them for you.

If you ask the speaker to use the words in sentences, the words will sound more natural. You can also ask speakers to record words and sentences so you can practice them again and again.

Exercise 7

Part A: Think about an upcoming class, meeting, presentation, or discussion. Write five words that you want to say clearly. Write the dictionary pronunciations.

Example: Yu Huang studies English. He could not think of an upcoming situation, but these words gave him trouble when he was looking at used cars: *mechanic, guarantee,* and *transmission.*

YOUR WORDS	DICTIONARY PRONUNCIATIONS
Example: mechanic	/mə ˈkæ nɪk/
1.	
2.	
3.	
4.	
5.	

Part B: Write a typical phrase or sentence you might use with each word from Exercise 7A. Dictate each sentence to your partner. Say it three times naturally. Look up from your book when you are speaking.

Example: (mechanic) Can I take it to a mechanic?

1. _____
2. _____
3. _____
4. _____
5. _____

Exercise 8

Write key technical or professional terms you use regularly at school or work. Circle the words with pronunciations you are not sure of. Look up the circled words and write the pronunciations.

	KEY TERMS	**DICTIONARY PRONUNCIATIONS**
Example:	receipt	/rə ˈsiʸt/
1.		
2.		
3.		
4.		
5.		
6.		
7.		
8.		
9.		
10.		

Speak in slow motion and say each word once, then twice in a row, and then three times in a row. Contribute one or two of the most difficult words from your list and create a class list of difficult words.

Pronunciation Guide for *Well Said, Third Edition*

The pronunciation symbols in *Well Said* are similar to the IPA symbols used in many dictionaries for learners of English. They are the same as the IPA symbols used in the *Newbury House Dictionary* except for four vowel sounds. Those sounds are shaded in the chart below.

As you look through the IPA symbols, notice that many symbols look like letters of the English alphabet; some do not. The symbols are printed between slanted lines (/) next to familiar key words. Complete the chart by writing the symbols *your* dictionary uses for each sound.

CD 1; Track 7 Learn to say the key words. Listen and repeat after your teacher or the speaker on audio.

Key Word	Consonant Symbols		
	Well Said	*Newbury Dictionary*	*Your Dictionary*
1. *p*ie	/p/	/p/	
2. *b*oy	/b/	/b/	
3. *t*en	/t/	/t/	
4. *d*ay	/d/	/d/	
5. *k*ey	/k/	/k/	
6. *g*o	/g/	/g/	
7. *f*ine	/f/	/f/	
8. *v*an	/v/	/v/	
9. *th*ink	/θ/	/θ/	
10. *th*ey	/ð/	/ð/	
11. *s*ee	/s/	/s/	
12. *z*oo	/z/	/z/	
13. *sh*oe	/ʃ/	/ʃ/	
14. mea*s*ure	/ʒ/	/ʒ/	
15. *ch*oose	/tʃ/	/tʃ/	
16. *j*ob	/dʒ/	/dʒ/	
17. *m*y	/m/	/m/	
18. *n*o	/n/	/n/	
19. si*ng*	/ŋ/	/ŋ/	
20. *l*et	/l/	/l/	
21. *r*ed	/r/	/r/	
22. *w*e	/w/	/w/	
23. *y*es	/y/	/y/	
24. *h*ome	/h/	/h/	

Vowel Sounds and Symbols			
Key Word	**Well Said**	**Newbury Dictionary**	**Your Dictionary**
1. h*e*	/iʸ/	/i/	
2. h*i*t	/ɪ/	/ɪ/	
3. m*ay*	/eʸ/	/eɪ/	
4. g*e*t	/ɛ/	/ɛ/	
5. m*a*d	/æ/	/æ/	
6. b*ir*d	/ɜr/	/ɜr/	
7. c*u*p	/ʌ/	/ʌ/	
*a*bout	/ə/	/ə/	
8. h*o*t, f*a*ther	/ɑ/	/ɑ/	
9. t*oo*	/uʷ/	/u/	
10. g*oo*d	/ʊ/	/ʊ/	
11. kn*ow*	/oʷ/	/oʊ/	
12. l*aw*	/ɔ/	/ɔ/	
13. f*i*ne	/aɪ/	/aɪ/	
14. n*ow*	/aʊ/	/aʊ/	
15. b*oy*	/ɔɪ/	/ɔɪ/	

*The vowel sounds in *cup* and <u>a</u>bout are similar sounds. The vowel sound/symbol in *cup* is used in stressed words and syllables while the vowel sound/symbol in <u>a</u>bout is used in unstressed words and syllables.

Exercise 9

Place the symbol from *Well Said* next to the underlined sound in each word. Compare your answers with your partner's answers.

Consonants

1. <u>ch</u>ips _____
2. <u>c</u>oupon _____
3. ri<u>ng</u> _____
4. tou<u>gh</u> _____
5. bro<u>th</u>er _____

Vowels

1. b<u>o</u>ss _____
2. ch<u>ee</u>secake _____
3. afr<u>ai</u>d _____
4. m<u>u</u>ch _____
5. f<u>oo</u>t _____

Exercise 10

The cartoon at the beginning of the chapter shows pronunciation symbols for *Zhevalski*, the last name of the football player. Write your first and last names below. Using phonetic symbols from *Well Said*, write the pronunciation of *your* name between the slanted lines. Ask your partner to use the symbols to pronounce your name.

First Name: ___Liza___ v·v·____ / ˈlɪ, ˈlay / ˈzl, ˈlay /

Last Name: ___Vivi_____ / vl, ˈlay / ˈvl, ˈay /

What sounds in your name do not exist in English?

You Choose!

Do you want an overview of consonant and/or vowel symbols?
  • *Go to Supplements 1-4 for consonants and 10–12 for vowels.*

Do you want to move on to sound/spelling patterns?
  • *Continue with Chapter 3.*

Consonant Sounds and Spellings

English has been influenced by many other languages. As a result, words do not always sound the way they are spelled, as illustrated in the "gila monster" cartoon below.

"It's pronounced 'hee-la' monster. The 'g' sounds like an 'h.'"

Notice how many different ways the letter *g* is pronounced in these words:

    gold   = /g/ as in **g**o

    generally = /dʒ/ as in **j**ob

    bei**g**e   = /ʒ/ as in mea**su**re

    gila   = /h/ as in **h**ome

Notice how many different spellings produce the same /ʃ/ sound as in **sh**oe:

    share = /ʃ/   ra**ti**o   = /ʃ/

    so**ci**al = /ʃ/   a**ss**ure = /ʃ/

    sugar = /ʃ/   ma**ch**ine = /ʃ/

Some pronunciation problems in English are related to difficulties in recognizing sound-spelling patterns. In this chapter, you will learn about sounds and spellings that are especially troublesome.

You will also learn how to pronounce final voiced and voiceless consonant sounds. Usually spelling offers clues about whether consonant sounds are voiceless (lea*f*) or voiced (lea*ve*), but not always. At the same time, you will discover the importance of final sounds and syllable length in English.

Listen!

CD 1; Track 8

Listening Activity 1

Listen to your teacher or the speaker on audio read a short passage. The first time, close your book and listen. The second time, listen to the sounds of the *italicized* letters.

AMERICAN GOVERNMENT

Many interna*ti*onal students are confused about the government of the United States. They wonder who makes the deci*si*ons. Is the power located in the presiden*ti*al office or in the congre*ssi*onal offices?

The answer goes back over two cen*tu*ries. Ever since the American Revolu*ti*on, Americans have been suspi*ci*ous of government power. Early Americans believed that England had abused its power and limited indivi*du*al freedom. They believed that the primary role of na*ti*onal government was to protect indivi*du*al freedom and to encourage self-suffi*ci*ency.

Due to the mistrust of strong central governments, the writers of the Constitu*ti*on divided power among three branches: executive (the president), legislative (the congress), and judi*ci*al (the courts). Although this divi*si*on may not be the most effi*ci*ent way to govern, it prevents any one branch from gaining too much power.

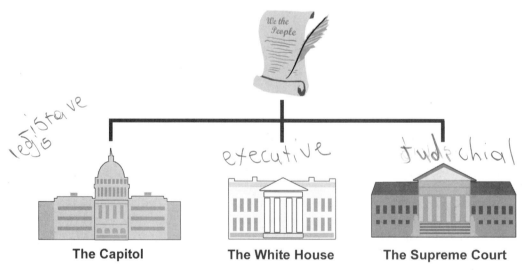

The Capitol   The White House   The Supreme Court

Organization chart of the United States government.

The passage contained several unusual sound/spelling patterns. What were some of the italicized sounds? In this chapter, you will discover pronunciation guidelines for the italicized spellings.

Listening Activity 2

Listen to the teacher or the speaker on audio say one phrase from each pair. Check the one you hear.

Example: _____ special pri**ce**   _____ special pri**z**e

1. _____ heavy ro**pe**   _____ heavy ro**b**e

2. _____ make a be**t**   _____ make a be**d**

3. _____ annual ra**ce**   _____ annual rai**s**e

4. _____ ba**ck** it up   _____ ba**g** it up

5. _____ small pie**ce**   _____ small pea**s**

6. _____ hear a bu**s**   _____ hear a bu**zz**

7. _____ bad sea**t**   _____ bad see**d**

8. _____ se**t** the example   _____ sai**d** the example

Check your answers.

Now listen to both phrases in each pair. Do you hear the difference?

Rules and Practices 1:
Unusual Consonant Spelling Patterns

The following spelling patterns are common in business, academic, medical, scientific, and technical terms. Like most guidelines, these will be true *most* of the time, not *all* of the time.

Rule 3-1

The /ʃ/ sound is commonly spelled *sh* as in **sh**oe.

Listen to the italicized letters in the phrases below. Circle the sound you hear in each column. Do you hear . . .

/t/ or /ʃ/?	/s/ or /ʃ/?	/s/ or /ʃ/?
slow mo*ti*on	so*ci*al life	first impre*ssi*on
our genera*ti*on	spe*ci*al price	environmental i*ssu*es
independent na*ti*on	finan*ci*al support	blood pre*ssu*re

✓ **Complete the Rule:** The *-ti-*, *-ci-*, *-ssi-*, and *-ssu-* in these suffixes or word endings are additional spellings for the /   / sound as in _____.

Rule 3-2

CD 1; Track 11

The /tʃ/ sound is commonly spelled *ch* as in ***ch***oose.
Listen to the italicized letters in the phrases. Circle the sound you hear. Do you hear . . .

/t/ or /tʃ/?

21st cen***tu***ry

fu***tu***re role

na***tu***ral resources

✔ **Complete the Rule:** The *-tu-* in suffixes and word endings is another spelling for the / / sound as in _____.

Exercise 1

The words below have been split into two parts. With a partner, join the parts back together and write each word in the correct column. The first two have been done.

Word Split			
Word Beginnings		*Word Endings*	
1. nego-	**5.** congra-	-cial	-ture ✔
2. litera-	**6.** tradi-	-tiate ✔	-tion
3. offi-	**7.** i-	-ssue	-tually
4. cen-	**8.** ac-	-tulate	-tury

/ʃ/
as in ***sh***oe

negotiate _____

_____

_____

_____

/tʃ/
as in ***ch***oose

literature _____

_____

_____

_____

CD 1; Track 12 Say the words after the teacher or the speaker on audio.

Notes for /tʃ/ as in ***ch***oose:

1. The *ch* spelling sounds like /ʃ/ as in ***sh***oe in *machine, chef, Chicago,* and *Michigan,* and like /k/ in ***k***ey in *architecture, chaos, chemical, chronic, stomachache, orchestra,* and *chlorine.*

2. (For advanced students) When *-n-* precedes *-ti-* (*attention, presidential, credentials*), the *-ti-* can be pronounced /ʃ/ in ***sh***oe or /tʃ/ in ***ch***oose.

Rule 3-3

CD 1; Track 13

The /ʒ/ as in mea**su**re rarely occurs at the beginning of words.
Listen to the italicized letters. Circle the sound you hear in each column. Do you hear . . .

/z/, /ʃ/, or /ʒ/?	/z/, /ʃ/, or /ʒ/?
difficult deci**si**on	security mea**su**re
perfect vi**si**on	lei**su**re travel
A**si**an countries	ca**su**al clothes

☑ **Complete the Rule:** The *-si-* and *-su-* in suffixes are common spellings for the / / sound as in _____. (*Pronunciation hint:* /ʃ/ + voicing* = /ʒ/)

Rule 3-4

CD 1; Track 14

The /dʒ/ sound is commonly spelled *j* as in **j**ob and *g* as in **g**eneral.
Listen to the italicized letters. Circle the sound that you hear. Do you hear . . .

/d/ or /dʒ/?

indivi**du**al interests
simple proce**du**re => grae·dʒu~it
gra**du**ate school

☑ **Complete the Rule:** In General American English, the *-du-* in the middle of words is another spelling for the / / sound as in _____.
(*Pronunciation hint:* /tʃ/ + voicing* = /dʒ/)

A Helpful Hint

The consonant sounds in **sh**oe, mea**su**re, **ch**oose, and **j**ob are difficult for many students. This chart summarizes the differences.

		VOICELESS	VOICED
Stream of air:		/ʃ/ in **sh**oe	/ʒ/ in mea**su**re
Burst of air:		/tʃ/ in **ch**oose	/dʒ/ in **j**ob

If you have trouble distinguishing between voiceless and voiced sounds, cup your hands over your ears. This emphasizes the vibration of the voiced sounds and makes them sound especially loud.

---

*voicing = vocal cord vibration

Exercise 2

With a partner, look at the italicized letters and say the words. Write the words
and phrases in the correct columns below.

ready to nego*ti*ate	even*tu*ally	interna*ti*onal students	government offi*ci*al
profe*ssi*onal sports	special occa*si*on	indivi*du*al differences	normal proce*du*re
my plea*su*re	busy sche*du*le	made a deci*si*on	human na*tu*re
double vi*si*on	early depar*tu*re	gra*du*al changes	21st cen*tu*ry

Column 1	**Column 2**	**Column 3**	**Column 4**
/ʃ/	/tʃ/	/ʒ/	/dʒ/
as in **sh**oe	as in **ch**oose	as in mea**su**re	as in **j**ob
negotati·	departure	pleasure	gradual Schuadele
professional	Nature	pleasure	individual
International	eventually	ocassion	Proceduare
official	Procedure	decision	eventually
		vision	

 Repeat each list of phrases after your teacher or the speaker on audio.

CD 1; Track 15

You Choose!

Do you want more pronunciation practice with /ʃ/ and /tʃ/?
- *Go to Supplement 7.*

Do you want to move on with sound/spelling practice?
- *Continue below.*

InfoGap

Exercise 3

In pairs, complete the crossword puzzle. *Student A* has half of the words for the
puzzle on page 207. *Student B* has the other half on page 208. Take turns saying the
words with the suffixes to your partner. Write the words in the puzzle. Do *not* look
in your partner's book.

Check the most difficult words to pronounce. Report them to your teacher. Practice them with your class.

Rule 3-5

CD 1; Track 16 Listen to the *qu* spelling pattern. Do you hear one or two sounds? Circle the sound(s) you hear. Do you hear . . .

/k/ or /kw/?

quick response

quality control

e***qu***al amount

☑ **Complete the Rule:** The *-qu-* and *qu-* spellings are pronounced like the two consonant sounds /   /. (*Pronunciation hint*: Round the lips for /w/ before you release the /k/ sound.)

More words with /kw/: *ade***qu***ate, se***qu***ence, li***qu***id, **qu***ality, **qu***antity, **qu***antify, **qu***alify, **qu***adrant.*

Rule 3-6

CD 1; Track 17

Listen to the *x* and *cc* spelling patterns. Do you hear one or two sounds? Circle the sound(s) you hear. Do you hear . . .

/s/ or /ks/?	/s/ or /ks/?
ex**tr**a effort	a**cc**ept responsibility
legal ex**p**ert	huge su**cc**ess
personal ex**p**erience	easy a**cc**ess

✔ **Complete the Rule:** The -*x*- and -*cc*- spellings are usually pronounced like the TWO sounds /   /.

Exercise 4

CD 1; Track 18

Repeat the sentences after your teacher or the speaker on audio. Or practice with a partner as follows.

Student B: Close your book. Your partner will tell you what to say.

Student A: Give Student B the starter phrase to memorize: *I know a good Web site that has . . .*

Student A says . . .   *Student B says . . .*

. . . office furniture   I know a good Web site that has office furniture.

. . . casual clothes   I know a good Web site that has casual clothes.

. . . natural vitamins   I know a good Web site that has natural vitamins.

Example: Starter Phrase   *Completion Phrases*

I know a good Web site that has . . .   office furni**tu**re.

casua l clothes.

nat**u**ral vitamins.

ed**u**ca**ti**onal software.

Note: The -*x*- in *example*, *exact*, *executive*, and *examine* is pronounced as a voiced /gz/.

Starter Phrase	*Completion Phrase*

1. When is the ne**x**t . . .

quiz?

quarterly meeting?

qualifying exam?

quality control meeting?

2. What is the si**tu**a**ti**on with . . .

your depar**tu**re?

the tempera**tu**re?

the fea**tu**red speaker?

our fu**tu**re role?

(Switch Roles)

3. Those were e**x**cellent . . .

deci**si**ons.

revi**si**ons.

mea**su**rements.

maps of A**si**a.

4. When did they sche**du**le . . .

gra**du**ation?

your proce**du**re?

the gra**du**ate student meeting?

our indivi**du**al conferences?

Something to Think About

In this class, you may be asked to monitor or listen carefully to the following:

- **A class member's (peer's) pronunciation while he or she is speaking.** If you hear a problem, don't interrupt. Just note it, and point it out when your partner finishes speaking. Give your partner the chance to correct the error.

- **Your pronunciation while you are speaking.** If you hear a problem while you are speaking, don't be discouraged. Noticing it is a sign of progress! Correct it or ask for help, if possible, or just move on.

- **Your recorded pronunciation.** Focus on one or two pronunciation points per recording. Listen for clear as well as unclear examples. When you hear a problem, stop the recording and note it. Then continue listening. At the end of the recording, make corrections and listen again.

Monitoring gets easier with practice. As your peer-monitoring improves, so will your self-monitoring.

Exercise 5

In circles of three or four, do a *round-robin reading* of "American Government" at the beginning of the chapter. In round-robin readings, each student takes a turn reading a sentence. When you are finished, repeat the activity with a different student reading the first sentence. Monitor your classmates' pronunciation of the italicized spellings.

Rules and Practices 2: Final Consonant Sounds and Spellings

Final consonant sounds are important. They make speech clear, but some students omit them. They might say *"bo- answers"* for *"both answers."* Other students confuse final voiceless and voiced consonants; they might say *"Half a good day!"* for *"Have a good day!"* Final consonants sounds are either voiceless or voiced.

No vibration of the vocal cords.   Vibration of the vocal cords.

English has eight consonant pairs that are almost the same except that one sound in each pair is voiceless and the other is voiced:

	Consonant Pair Sounds	Other Consonant Sounds
Voiceless	/p t k f θ s ʃ tʃ/	/h/
Voiced	/b d g v ð z ʒ dʒ/	/m n ŋ l r w y/

Often spelling signals whether a consonant is voiceless or voiced:

    bus   /bʌs/

    buzz   /bʌz/

Sometimes it does not:

    close friends   /kloʷs/

    close the door   /kloʷz/

Do you want an overview of voiced and voiceless consonants?
  • *See Supplement 2.*

Do you want to practice *final* voiced and voiceless consonants?
  • *Continue below.*

Rule 3-7

CD 1; Track 19

Listen to the final voiceless and voiced consonant sounds. Can you hear a difference?

VOICELESS	VOICED
whi**te**	wi**de**
whi**te** beaches	wi**de** beaches
nea**t**	nee**d**
nea**t** space	nee**d** space
ro**pe**	ro**be**
tied the ro**pe**	tied the ro**be**
pri**ce**	pri**ze**
best pri**ce**	best pri**ze**
sa**fe**	sa**ve**
sa**fe** neighborhoods	sa**ve** neighborhoods

CD 1; Track 20

The difference between final voiceless and voiced consonants can be hard to hear. The most obvious difference is in the preceding vowel.

✔ **Complete the Rule:** Vowels sound longer before final (voiceless/voiced) consonants.

Examples:

VOICELESS	VOICED
short *vowel*	***lo—o—onger*** *vowel*
la**p**	la—**b**
le**t**	le—**d**
lo**ck**	lo—**g**
bu**s**	bu—**zz**
lea**f**	lea—**ve**

Exercise 6

CD 1; Track 21 Listen to the teacher or the speaker on audio say the sentences. Fill in the blanks with the sounds that you hear. Or do a partner dictation as follows:

Student A: Write the sound you intend to say in front of the sentence. Say the sentence to *Student B.*

Student B: Fill in each blank with the sound you hear.

/p/ or /b/?

1. _____ Your notebook is in your la_____.

2. _____ I'm afraid this ro _____ e is worn out.

3. _____ I couldn't find a ca_____.

/t/ or /d/?

1. _____ They generally spen_____ Saturday in the library.

2. _____ Did you make the be _____?

3. _____ Take the car_____ to the checkout.

/k/ or /g/?

1. _____ Be careful when you ba _____ it up.

2. _____ Those are huge lo _____ s.

3. _____ Nice to meet you, Professor Bu _____. (Buck or Bugg)

CD 1; Track 21 Check your answers. Repeat the sentences. If you are working with a partner, check your answers and switch roles.

Something to Think About

In North American English, the voiceless /t/ sometimes sounds like a quick voiced /d/.

Examples:	metal	*sounds like*	medal
	city	*sounds like*	cidy
	right away	*sounds like*	ride away
	great idea	*sounds like*	grade idea

The /t/ is pronounced like a quick /d/ when /t/ is between vowel sounds and the next syllable is unstressed. It is important for you to recognize this sound change when you listen to North American English.

Rule 3-8

CD 1; Track 22 The following word pairs are spelled the same but pronounced differently. What is the difference in pronunciation?

NOUNS/ADJECTIVES	VERBS
use	use
close	close
excuse	excuse
abuse	abuse

In which column are the vowels longer? In which column are the final sounds voiced?

✔ **Complete the Rule:** In the words above, the final consonants are (voiceless/voiced) in nouns and adjectives. They are (voiceless/voiced) in verbs.

Exercise 7

CD 1; Track 23 Repeat the phrases after the speaker on audio. Or practice with your teacher. If your teacher says a phrase from the first column ("half a cookie"), say the pair phrase from the second column ("have a cookie"), and vice versa.

The vowels in the second column should be about 1½ times as long as the vowels in the first column.

NOUNS/ADJECTIVES	VERBS
short preceding vowel	*lo—o—onger* preceding vowel
1. half a cookie	have a cookie
2. belief in your ability	believe in your ability
3. safe money	save money
4. advice about finances	advise about finances
5. relief from pain	relieve from pain
6. loose change	lose change
7. use in the kitchen	use in the kitchen
8. close windows	close windows
9. house guests	house guests
10. excuse from class	excuse from class

Exercise 8

Listen carefully as your teacher or the speaker on audio says each sentence twice. Do you hear the italicized word? Circle the word you hear.

Example: That's a *wide* door. (wide) white

1.	Have a *safe* trip.	safe	save
2.	I *need* two pounds of fish.	need	neat
3.	I can't *believe* it.	believe	belief
4.	Can you *prove* it?	prove	proof
5.	*Leave* the key at the desk.	leave	leaf
6.	They let us *feed* the fish.	feed	feet
7.	Would you *close* the door?	/z/ close	/s/ close
8.	His notebook's in his *lab*.	lab	lap
9.	Would you *excuse* me?	/z/ excuse	/s/ excuse
10.	I'll *have* a cup of coffee.	have	half

Check your answers with your teacher. With a partner, take turns saying the above sentences. Monitor your partner.

A Helpful Hint

How do you address women in the United States?

Miss	= /mɪs/, for unmarried women
Ms.	= /mɪz/, for married or unmarried women
Missus (Mrs.)	= /mɪsɪz/, for married women

These titles are used before a woman's last or family name. Many women prefer the general title Ms. to Miss or Mrs. because Ms. can be used without regard to marital status. Ms. is also the correct title for a married woman who keeps her own name after marriage.

Exercise 9

CD 1; Track 25 Listen to your teacher or the speaker on audio say titles and names. Check *Married* if you hear Mrs., *Single* if you hear Miss, and *Don't Know* if you hear Ms. Remember that Ms., with the final voiced /z/, sounds almost twice as long as Miss, with the final voiceless /s/.

Mrs. – Married	Miss – Single	Ms. – Don't Know
Example		✔
1.		
2.		
3.		
4.		
5.		
6.		
7.		

Check your answers with your teacher.

Communicative Practice: Evacuate!

You must leave your home and go to a safe shelter in a local school because of a hurricane. You have only fifteen minutes to gather essential items from your home. In a moment, you and your "family" will choose seven items to take with you. Your family includes a grandfather, a wife, a husband, a seven-year-old son, and an eight-month-old daughter.

Step 1: Preview Pronunciation

Practice the sound/spelling patterns in these useful phrases:

We have to make a deci**si**on . . .

That's not essen**ti**al . . .

We nee**d** / don't nee**d** . . .

I think / don't think we'**d** use . . .

Preview the sound/spelling patterns in these words from the evacuation list:
medica**ti**on, in**su**rance, televi**si**on, bo**x**

Preview the final consonants in these words from the evacuation list:
ca**t**, foo**d**, i-Po**d**, first-ai**d** ki**t**, clothe**s** /klo^wz/, flashligh**t**.

Step 2: Rank Items Individually

Listed below are items you may want to take with you. Take five minutes and individually rank the seven most important items (1 = most essential; 2 = next most essential; and so on). Be prepared to give reasons for your choices.

Evacuation List	Personal Ranking	Family Ranking
Cat		
Cat food		
Flashlight		
Grandfather's medication		
Clothes		
Battery-powered television		
First-aid kit		
Insurance papers		
Diapers		
Candles		
Canned food		
Can opener		
Games/books for recreation		
Box of matches		
Baby food		
i-Pod		

Step 3: Achieve Agreement

In the remaining ten minutes, share your individual rankings in groups of five students. Try to reach an agreement as a "family" about what to take. Report your top choices and some reasons to the class.

A Helpful Hint

Unlearning old habits and learning new ones take time. These strategies will make your out-of-class consonant practice more effective.

1. **Focus on the feel** of the new sounds. Practice silently and s-l-o-w-l-y. Mouth the beginning, middle, and end of words. Then say the words out loud.
2. **Focus on the sound** of the new pattern. Practice with your eyes closed.
3. **Focus on the look** of the new sounds. Practice in front of a mirror. Imitate the facial positions and mouth movements of proficient English speakers. Clear English pronunciation requires active use of the mouth, lips, and jaw.

Keep a list of difficult words you want to learn. Review them frequently, using these strategies. Practice the words in typical phrases and sentences you would say in real situations. Imagine that you are an actor rehearsing before you go onstage.

Prime-Time Practice

See the Oral Review on the next page. Read it silently for meaning. Then read the passage out loud. Write the five most difficult words or phrases:

1. _____
2. _____
3. _____
4. _____
5. _____

Practice the words/phrases, using the strategies in *A Helpful Hint* above. Which strategies do you think were most helpful to you? _____

_____

Oral Review: Sound and Spelling Patterns

Name: _____ Date: _____

Directions: You are a member of a nonprofit group that educates the public about environmental issues. You have been asked to tape a public service broadcast. Practice and then record the announcement below.

Public Service Announcement

Good evening, everyone.

Earth Day 1990 called the world's ***attention*** to the ***future*** of our environment. Here are some of the most serious threats facing the planet and some things ***individuals*** can do to save it.

Scientists are ***expressing*** concern about the greenhouse effect, the ***gradual*** warming of the earth due to the growth of greenhouse-like gases. The increase in ***temperatures*** is causing ***glaciers*** to melt and sea levels to ***rise***. What can we do? Buy energy-***efficient*** appliances and ***drive*** fuel-***efficient*** cars.

Another problem is garbage and the ***pollution*** of groundwater. ***Individuals*** can respond to this ***issue*** by recycling newspapers, cans, glass, and plastic. They can also persuade local governments to increase fines for industrial ***pollution*** in streams and rivers.

This is the first in our series of ***special*** announcements called "What on Earth Can We Do?" Help us with ***future*** broadcasts. Tell us what people like you are doing to protect the environment for the next ***generation***. Call 555-2000 and leave a 60-second message on our ***machine***.

Directions for Recording: Listen to your recording. Check your pronunciation of all italicized words. Make corrections at the end. Submit the recording to your teacher. (See Appendix A, page 215 for recording suggestions.)

Syllables and Word Endings

CD 1; Track 26

Words in English have one or more syllables, or beats. Listen to the words below. How many beats do you hear in each word?

act	active	actively	activity
late	relate	related	relationship

Now say the words with your teacher, and tap the syllables as beats on your desk.

tap	*tap*	*tap*	*tap*	*tap*	*tap*	*tap*	*tap*	*tap*	*tap*
act		ac	tive	ac	tive	ly	ac	ti	vi	ty
late		re	late	re	la	ted	re	la	tion	ship

Students learning English sometimes drop syllables or add syllables. Dropping or adding syllables can make speech hard to understand. In this chapter, you will learn the importance of syllables and word endings.

Listen!

Listening Activity 1

CD 1; Track 27

Listen to the teacher or speaker on audio say a phrase from each pair. Check the one you hear. Then, check your answers with your teacher.

Examples: _____ used to cook   ✔ use it to cook

    ✔ official quotes   _____ official quotas

1. ✔ planned a garden   ✔ planted a garden
2. _____ canned a salmon   ✔ Canada salmon
3. ✔ former states   ✔ former status
4. ✔ need to know   _____ needed to know
5. ✔ explained to me   ✔ explain it to me
6. ✔ Miss Smith   _____ Mrs. Smith
7. ✔ keep the notes   ✔ keep the notice
8. _____ the tasks   ✔ the task is . . .
9. ✔ see the difference   ✔ see the differences
10. ✔ perfect hosts   _____ perfect hostess

CD 1; Track 28

Listen to the teacher or speaker on the audio say both phrases. What is the difference between the phrases in each pair?

CD 1; Track 29
Close your book and listen to a reading about color preference. The speaker will consistently omit an essential feature of English pronunciation. What is missing?*

CD 1; Track 30
Now listen to the passage with -s endings. Fill in as many blanks as you can.

COLOR PREFERENCE

For many ___years___, people have been researching the ___factors___ that influence color preference. The ___results___ are open to question, but they have been used to make ___decisicions/decisions___ about ___colors___ used in decorating, fashion, Web design, and the packaging of consumer ___goods___.

One factor that ___influences___ color choice is age. ___babies___ are attracted to bright, warm ___colors___ like yellow and red. ___adults___, on the other hand, prefer cool ___colors___ like blue and green.

Where people live also ___Affects___ color preference. Often a home ___reflécts___ a color break from the outside environment. The brown scenery in the Southwest ___offers___ little color, so ___houses___ there have pink, orange, and other bright ___colors___. In industrial ___cities___ of the North, people like white ___curtains___ in reaction to industrial smoke and dirt.

Finally, personality ___Affects___ color choice. A person who ___likes___ red is athletic and extroverted. Someone who ___preffes___ orange is friendly; a person who ___preffers___ pink is feminine and charming; and, a person who ___loves___ blue is intellectual and conservative. According to recent research, blue is the best-liked color across ___cultures___.

Dictate to your teacher the words you wrote in the blanks. Notice how **frequently** -s endings occur.

Listening Activity 3

Listen to your teacher or the speaker on audio say one phrase from each pair.
Check the one you hear.

CD 1; Track 31

1. _____ John's answer   _____ John answers.

2. _____ the baby's smile   _____ The baby smiles.

3. _____ My brother works.   _____ My brothers work.

4. _____ Ann's dance   _____ Ann dances.

5. _____ His friends help.   _____ His friend helps.

Check your answers. Discuss the differences in meaning.

Rules and Practices 1:
Syllables and -s Endings

We use -s endings on the following:

Plurals: My brother**s** work.

Verbs (present tense singular): My brother work**s**.

Possessives: What was Ann**'s** answer?

Contractions: The battery**'s** dead.

Most -s endings are sounds:

tap	*tap*
debt	debts
serve	serves

Sometimes -s endings are syllables:

tap	*tap - tap*
loss	loss - es
fix	fix - es

Rule 4-1

CD 1; Track 32

We pronounce the -s ending in one of three ways. Listen and write what the -s ending sounds like in each group.

1. fit/fits   work/works   Mark/Mark's   = _____

2. pay/pays   read/reads   Laura/Laura's   = _____

3. teach/teaches   office/offices George/George's = _____

✔ Compare your answers with these rules:

1. *If the word ends in a voiceless sound (fi<u>t</u>, wor<u>k</u>, Mar<u>k</u>), add the voiceless /s/ — a hissing sound.*

2. *If the word ends in a voiced sound (pa<u>y</u>, rea<u>d</u>, Laur<u>a</u>), add the voiced /z/ — a buzzing sound.*

3. *If the word already ends in a hissing or buzzing sound (offi<u>ce</u>, Geor<u>ge</u>), add the syllable /əz/ or /ɪz/.*

Examples of words that end in hissing or buzzing (sibilant) sounds:

tap	*tap*	*- tap*
/s/ mi<u>ss</u>	miss	- es
/z/ si<u>ze</u>	siz	- es
/ʃ/ pu<u>sh</u>	push	- es
/tʃ/ wa<u>tch</u>	watch	- es
/dʒ/ ju<u>dge</u>	judg	- es

Exercise 1

CD 1; Track 33

Say the word pairs below with the teacher or the speaker on audio. Write the number of syllables in each pair.

Final /əz/ Syllable		**Final /s/ Sound**		**Final /z/ Sound**	
source/sources	(1 / 2)	lock/locks	(1 / 1)	role/roles	(1 / 1)
page/pages	(/)	hope/hopes	(/)	Steve/Steve's	(/)
class/classes	(/)	minute/minutes	(/)	item/items	(/)
Rose/Rose's	(/)	stop/stops	(/)	grade/grades	(/)
college/colleges	(/)	headache/headaches	(/)	policy/policies	(/)
difference/differences	(/)	ticket/tickets	(/)	copy/copies	(/)

Exercise 2

With a partner, add an *-s* ending to each word and say it. Decide whether you added a sound or a syllable and write the verb in the correct column.

Word	Add a Sound	Add a Syllable
1. dance	-S	dances
2. leave	leaves	
3. use	uses	uses
4. plan		
5. job	Jobs	
6. improve	Improves	
7. analyze	Analyzes	
8. estimate	Stimates	
9. finish		finishes
10. assume		

Check your answers with your teacher.

Watch
wash

CD 1; Track 34 Say the words in each column after the teacher or the speaker on audio. Then choose three useful words with *-s* endings and create sentences you might say. Take turns practicing the sentences. Monitor your partner.

1. _____

2. _____

3. _____

Exercise 3

CD 1; Track 35 Say the word pairs with the speaker on audio. Or work with a partner as follows: *Student A:* Say a word from Column A or B. *Student B:* Say the pair word.

Example: Student A: "cases"
Student B: "case"

A	B		A	B
1. case	cases		**6.** notice	notices
2. piece	pieces		**7.** tens	tennis
3. hosts	hostess		**8.** states	status
4. mailbox	mailboxes		**9.** quotes	quotas
5. folks	focus		**10.** pairs	Paris

Switch roles and repeat the exercise.

Exercise 4

Say the statements and responses with the speakers on audio. Or practice with a partner.

Student A: Say statement **a.** or **b.** Monitor your partner's response.
Student B: Cover the statements. Give the matching response.

STATEMENTS (STUDENT A)	RESPONSES (STUDENT B)

1. a. The *tire's* flat.   Which *one*?
   b. The *tires* are flat.   Which *ones*?

2. a. I helped the *hosts.*   They needed it.
   b. I helped the *hostess.*   She needed it.

3. a. He *let* her borrow his car.   Yesterday.
   b. He *lets* her borrow his car.   Every day.

4. a. Do you have the *notice?*   I have it.
   b. Do you have the *notices?*   I have them.

5. a. He missed his *chance* to make up the test.   And he had only one.
   b. He missed his *chances* to make up the test. And he had three!

6. a. They found your *suitcase.*   Where was it?
   b. They found your *suitcases.*   Where were they?

7. a. Her name is *Miss* Smith.   She's single?
   b. Her name is *Mrs.* Smith.   She's married?

8. a. What do I owe you for the *ticket?*   It was $15.00.
   b. What do I owe you for the *tickets?* They were $60.00.

9. a. My *cousin works* at the airport.   What does he do?
   b. My *cousins work* at the airport. What do they do?

10. a. Would you check the *mailbox?*   Which *one*?
    b. Would you check the *mailboxes?* Which *ones*?

Switch roles and repeat the exercise.

A Helpful Hint

Words that end in two consonant sounds can be difficult to pronounce (e.g., accept, test). Adding a final /s/ makes them even more difficult (e.g., acce**pts**, te**sts**). This is how English speakers simplify some consonant groups with *-s.*

1. Many English words end in *-ct* (fa**ct**), *-pt* (conce**pt**), and *-nd* (frie**nd**). When *-s* is added, English speakers generally omit the middle /t/ or /d/: fac̸ts, concep̸ts, and frienɗs.

2. Other English words end in *-st* (li**st**) and *-sk* (a**sk**). When *-s* is added, speakers *sometimes* omit the middle /t/ or /k/ and lengthen the /s/: lis̸ts, and as̸ks. This simplification is more common in rapid, casual speech.

Exercise 5

Part A: Repeat the words and phrases. In the phrases, notice the smooth connection or *link* between the final -s and the next word.

/kt+s/ = /ks/	/pt+s/ = /ps/	/nd+z/ = /nz/
fact/fac̸ts (sounds like *fax*)	adapt/adap̸ts	send/sen̸ds
fac̸ts‿of life	adap̸ts‿to the changes	sen̸ds‿a clear message
act/ac̸ts (sounds like *ax*)	concept/concep̸ts	lend/len̸ds
ac̸ts‿of kindness	some simple concep̸ts	len̸ds‿a hand
direct/direc̸ts	accept/accep̸ts	friend/frien̸ds
direc̸ts‿the project	accep̸ts‿responsibility	a few close frien̸ds

Part B: These same consonant groups can occur across word boundaries. Repeat.

1. They should accep̸t‿some responsibility.
2. Can you len̸d‿some money to my brother?
3. I need to fin̸d‿some family photographs.
4. Sen̸d‿some postcards from your trip.
5. He's been in China for the pas̸t‿six months.

Exercise 6

Part A: Do you hear careful or casual, rapid pronunciation? Circle the one you hear. (The symbol /:/ means that the previous sound is held a little longer.)

1. These (desks, /dɛs:/) are too small.   Careful / (Casual)
2. The book (lists, /lɪs:/) some examples.   Careful / Casual
3. She never (asks, /æs:/) for our homework.   Careful / Casual
4. Did the (guests, /gɛs:/) leave?   Careful / Casual
5. Have the (tests, /tɛs:/) been graded?   Careful / Casual

Check your answers.

Part B: Dictation. The teacher or the speaker on audio will say each sentence two times.

1. _____Who's our guest speaker?_____ (sounds like *Who's our guess speaker?*)
2. _____
3. _____
4. _____
5. _____

Check your answers with your teacher.

Exercise 7

Proverbs are short sayings that teach lessons. As general truths, proverbs are often expressed in the present tense. Underline the nouns and verbs ending in -s.

Say the proverbs with the teacher or speaker on audio. Or take turns saying the proverbs with a partner.

CD 1; Track 41

PROVERBS	MEANINGS
_d_ 1. Absence <u>makes</u> the heart grow fonder.	a. It is better to show than to tell.
_e_ 2. When life gives you lemons, make lemonade.	b. Time passes quickly when you are enjoying yourself.
_f_ 3. The early bird catches the worm.	c. Many projects require a community.
_g_ 4. No news is good news.	d. A lack of something increases your desire for it.
_h_ 5. Haste makes waste.	e. Make the best of what you are given in life.
_c_ 6. It takes a village.	f. Success comes to those who put in effort.
_b_ 7. Time flies when you are having fun.	g. Bad news travels faster than good news.
_a_ 8. Actions speak louder than words.	h. If we do things quickly, we make mistakes.

With a small group, match each proverb with the meaning. Which proverb do you like the best? Write it below. Talk about why you like it.

9. _____

Now translate a proverb from your language. Write it below.

Example of a Japanese proverb: The bamboo that <u>bends</u> is stronger than the oak that <u>resists</u>.

10. _____

Underline nouns or verbs ending with -s. Practice your proverb and share it with your group. What lesson or value does it teach?

Rules and Practices 2:
Syllables and *-ed* Endings

We use *-ed* endings primarily on regular verbs. The *-ed* ending affects meaning.

Present	**Past**
They **watch** a lot of old movies.	They **watched** a lot of old movies.
Most *-ed* endings are sounds:	Sometimes *-ed* endings are syllables:

tap	*tap*		*tap*	*tap - tap*
close	closed		wait	wait - ed
look	looked		end	end - ed

Rule 4-2

CD 1; Track 42

We pronounce the *-ed* ending on regular verbs in one of three ways. Listen and write what the *-ed* sounds like in these sentences.

1. They work hard.
They work**ed** hard.   = _____

2. The labs close at eight.
The labs clos**ed** at eight.   = _____

3. I wait for the bus.
I wait**ed** for the bus.   = _____

☑ Compare your answers with these rules:

1. *In verbs that end in voiceless sounds (wor<u>k</u>), the -ed sounds like the voiceless /t/.*

2. *In verbs that end in voiced sounds (clo<u>se</u>), the -ed sounds like the voiced /d/.*

3. *In verbs that end in /t/ or /d/ (wai<u>t</u>, a<u>dd</u>), the -ed sounds like the syllable /əd/ or /ɪd/.*

Exercise 8

CD 1; Track 43

Say the verb pairs below with your teacher or the speaker on audio. Write the number of syllables in each pair.

Final Syllable /əd/		Final Sound /t/		Final Sound /d/	
start/started	(1 / 2)	watch/watched	(1 / 1)	cause/caused	(1 / 1)
add/added	(1 / 2)	guess/guessed	(1 / 1)	save/saved	(1 / 1)
count/counted	(2 / 2)	check/checked	(1 / 1)	explain/explained	(1 / 2)
decide/decided	(1 / 3)	laugh/laughed	(1 / 1)	assume/assumed	(1 / 2)
expect/expected	(1 / 3)	finish/finished	(1 / 1)	realize/realized	(1 / 2)

Exceptions to Rule 4-2: Add the syllable /əd/ or /ɪd/ to a group of old-fashioned adjectives ending in *-ed*: nak-ed, wick-ed, crook-ed, wretch-ed, rag-ged, rug-ged, learn-ed, bless-ed, ag-ed. Add the syllable /əd/ or /ɪd/ to adverbs ending in *-edly*: sup-pos-ed-ly, al-leg-ed-ly, advis-ed-ly.

Exercise 9

Add an -*ed* ending to each verb and say it. Decide whether you added a sound or a syllable and write the verb in the correct column.

Word	Add a Sound	Add a Syllable
1. change	changed	
2. paint		painted
3. fix		
4. improve		
5. thank		
6. suggest		
7. ignore		
8. consider		
9. affect		
10. promise		

CD 1; Track 44

Check your answers.

Say the words in each column after your teacher or the speaker on audio.

Then choose three useful verbs with -*ed* endings and create sentences you might say. Take turns saying the sentences. Monitor your partner.

1. _____

2. _____

3. _____

A Helpful Hint

Linking or connecting words makes your speech smooth and natural. It sometimes makes word endings easier to pronounce.

We usually link the -*ed* ending with the next word in the phrase.

1. When the next word begins with a vowel sound, the -*ed* ending is clear and easy to hear.

We phoned in our order.   *sounds like*   We phone-din our order.

2. When the next word begins with a consonant sound, the -*ed* ending is sometimes hard to hear.

It worked just fine.   *sounds like*   It work just fine.

Exercise 10

With a partner, take turns saying the sentences. Link the *-ed* endings to the next word. *Note:* Two sentences have *-ed* endings that get lost.

1. That was already pointed out.
2. Carlos majored in economics.
3. I need something called a USB drive for my computer.
4. You'd better get that checked out.
5. The teacher doesn't expect that to be handed in.
6. They used to be apartments; now they're condos.
7. He already filled out the form and turned it in.
8. I went back and looked at my notes.
9. *Harry Potter* turned out to be a great movie.
10. Which countries refused to sign the treaty?

Which sentences had *-ed* endings that were difficult to hear?

CD 1; Track 45 Now repeat the sentences above after your teacher or the speaker on audio.

Communicative Practice: Two Truths and a "Tale"

USEFUL PAST TENSE VERBS			
started	attended	realized	increased
completed	planned	worked	conducted
graduated	studied	volunteered	coordinated
received	evaluated	served	visited
helped	coached	played	performed
managed	organized	avoided	moved

Use the verbs in the box to create three statements about your past education, employment, or free-time activities. Two statements should be true, and one should be false.

Example: ___I've played on a professional soccer team.___

Statement 1: ___I've visited MIT last year.___

Statement 2: ___I've studied physicology in this university___

Statement 3: ___I've performed breast dance last week.___

In small groups of four or five, say your statements to the group. Group members should write the statement they think is false and then compare their guesses. Monitor *-ed* endings.

Prime-Time Practice

Past Tense Narrative

A short story that teaches a lesson is called a *fable*. Fables were told by the ancient Greeks, and they are still told today. In this fable, you will practice *-ed* endings.

Step 1: Read the fable silently. Link (‿) the *-ed* endings.

The Man with Two Wives

In the days when men were **allowed** to have many wives, a middle-aged man had one young wife and one old one. Each **loved** him very much and **desired** to see him like herself. Now the man's hair was turning gray, which the young wife did not like because it made him look too old to be her husband. So every night she **combed** his hair and **picked** out the white strands. The elder wife saw her husband growing old with great pleasure, for she didn't like to be mistaken for his mother. So every morning she **arranged** his hair and **picked** out as many black strands as she could. As a result, the man soon found himself entirely bald.

Moral: Yield to all, and you will soon have nothing to yield. => given

Step 2: Record yourself reading the fable.

Step 3: Listen to your recording. Circle any verbs with *-ed* that you are not satisfied with. Re-record the phrases with those verbs. Send the recording to your teacher for feedback.

Extension (for advanced students): Write all verbs with *-ed* on an index card. Use the verbs to tell the story in your own words. Monitor the recording for verbs with *-ed* and smooth linking.

Exercise 11

TOEFL® iBT Speaking Practice (*Optional*)

One of the speaking tasks on the TOEFL® iBT often involves talking about an important person, place, or experience in your life. To do well on this type of task, you may need to describe or narrate in the past tense and use *-ed* endings.

1. Have available a watch with a second hand and equipment to record yourself.

2. Take about 15 seconds to prepare a response to the question in the box. You may use the outline below to help organize your thoughts.

3. Take about 45 seconds to respond.

> *Question:* Name one person outside of your family who has had the most influence on your life. Provide details and examples to support your choice.

Suggested outline:

Person's name: _____

Person's background: _____

_____

How/when you met this person: _____

_____

Reason/Examples 1: _____

2: _____

3: _____

4. Listen to your recording. Pay special attention to *-ed* endings.

5. For more practice, answer the same question except discuss "a person *in* your family," "a book," or "an event" that has had the most influence on your life.

Extend Your Skills . . . to Descriptions of Graphs

"This is the path to adulthood. You're here."

Explaining tables and graphs is a useful academic and business skill. When explaining information in graph form, we frequently use *-s* endings.

Step 1: Preview the five parts of your explanation and practice useful phrases.

Parts	Useful phrases with *-s* endings
a. Subject of the Graph	This graph **shows** . . . This graph **illustrates** . . .
b. Components of the Graph	The *x* (horizontal) axis **represents** . . . The *y* (vertical) axis **indicates** . .
c. Patterns	This graph **demonstrates** . . . One of the **trends** is . . . As _____ **increases**, . . . As _____ **decreases**, . . .
d. Example	For example, . . . For instance, . . .
e. Predictions or Implications	If this pattern (trend) **continues** . . . If this trend **holds** . . . One of the **conclusions** is . . . One of the **implications** is . . .

Note: When talking about trends, increases, and decreases, words like *slight(ly), gradual(ly), sharp(ly), dramatic(ally), and significant(ly)* are useful.

Step 2: Choose a graph from the following pages. Or find a clear, interesting graph of your own. Spend five minutes outlining a short explanation. Present the explanation to a small group or the class. Use notes or an outline; do not read.

Step 3: For homework, record your explanation. Listen to and evaluate your recording or the recording of a partner. Use the form on p. 51. Submit the recording and the form to your teacher.

Explaining A Graph/Self or Peer Evaluation Form

Name: _____ Date: _____

Part 1. Listen to the tape. Write down every noun and verb with an -s ending.

Part 2. Assign 1 point for each part of the explanation below. You might need to listen to the tape several times.

A. Organization   1 point each

    1. Subject clearly stated   _____

    2. Each component identified   _____

    3. Patterns/trends identified   _____

    4. One example given   _____

    5. End clearly indicated   _____

            (Part A) _____ $\times$ 10 = _____

B. Pronunciation   1 point each

    1. Adequate volume   _____

    2. Good speed   _____

    3. Clear key words   _____

    4. Final -s about 60%–75% accurate _____

    5. Good overall clarity   _____

            (Part B) _____ $\times$ 10 = _____

            TOTAL (Part A + B) = _____%

Comments:

_____

_____

_____

_____

_____

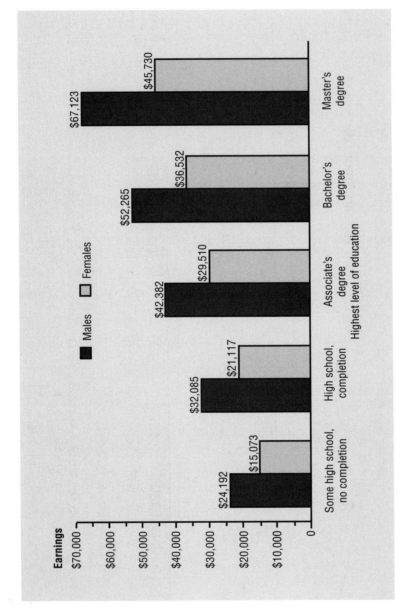

▲ Median annual income of persons 25 years old and over, by highest level of education and sex: 2002.

Source: U.S. Department of Commerce, Census Bureau, Current Population Reports, Series P-60. "Money Income in the United States: 2002."

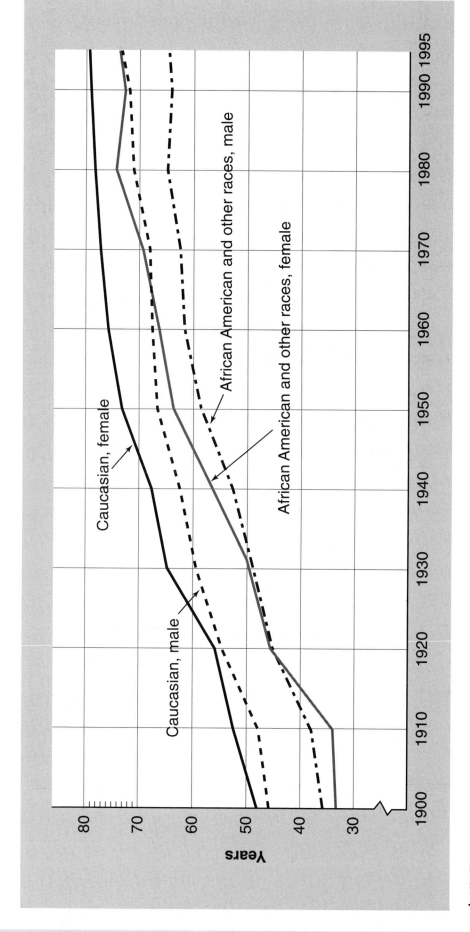

▲ Life Expectancy at Birth by Gender: United States, 1900–2000.

Sources: Vital Statistics of the United States 1973, vol. 2, part A, section 5 (U.S. Census Bureau; U.S. Department of Health, Education and Welfare, Public Health Service, National Center for Health Statistics); *Monthly Vital Statistics Report*, vol. 45, no. 11(S)2 (June 12, 1997), Centers for Disease Control and Prevention, 19.

Suggestion: Look up the life expectancy for people in the country where you were born. *See World Factbook* at https://www.cia.gov/cia/publications/factbook/index.html.

Oral Review: Syllables and Word Endings

Name: _____ Date: _____

Schedule an individual consultation with your teacher, submit a recording, or do the review as a pair project in which you dictate your completed sentences to your partner.

Complete each statement orally in any way that you choose. Do *not* write and then read your sentence completions.

1. The interviewer ask**ed** me if I have ever . . .

. . . been fire**d**.

. . . work**ed** on a team.

. . . manage**d** employees.

2. As soon as Edward gets home from work, he always . . .

3. Julie moved to Canada ten years ago, but she still . . .

4. Today people communicate by e-mail and cell phones; twenty-five years ago . . .

5. As soon as he arrived at the hotel, he . . .

6. Dr. Weeks never sees students in the morning; he . . .

7. He lives near the subway and doesn't drive, so he . . .

8. I didn't think the rent included any utilities, but it . . .

Listen to the recording. Monitor -*s* and -*ed* endings. Make corrections at the end of your recording.

Stress in Words

In words with two or more syllables, one syllable is stronger than the others. That syllable has primary *stress*.

TAP - tap	**tap - TAP**	**tap - TAP - tap**	**tap - TAP - tap - tap**
FI - nal	be - GIN	pro - FES - sor	pho - TO - gra - phy

What makes a syllable sound stressed in English?

The vowel in the stressed syllable is **clear**.

FI-nal

The stressed syllable often has a **higher pitch**.

FI-nal

Most important, the vowel in the stressed syllable is **longer**.

FI-nal

Listeners depend on stress to help them identify words. The more frequently you misuse stress, the more effort listeners have to make to understand you. The next two chapters will improve your ability to predict and use word stress.

Listen!

Listening Activity 1

CD 2; Track 1   Listen to the teacher or speaker on audio say one of the words from each pair. Check the word you hear. Then, check your answers with your teacher.

Example: ✔ greenhouse   _____ green house

1. _____ cities   _____ CDs
2. _____ selfish   _____ sell fish
3. _____ differentiated   _____ different shaded
4. _____ decade   _____ decayed
5. _____ pronouns   _____ pronounce
6. _____ desert   _____ dessert
7. _____ foremen   _____ for men
8. _____ one person   _____ one percent
9. _____ lookout   _____ Look out!
10. _____ homesick (sick *for* home)   _____ home sick (sick *at* home)

Now listen to *both* items in each pair. Can you hear the difference between them?

Something to Think About

If you stress the *wrong* syllable, you might be misunderstood.

Example: one PERcent   *might sound like*   one PERson

If you give syllables *equal* stress, you might be misunderstood.

Example: TU-TORS   *might sound like*   TWO TOURS

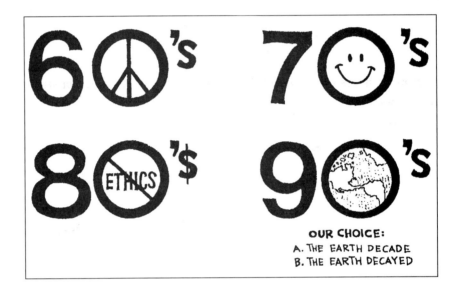

Listening Activity 2

CD 2; Track 3

Listen to the teacher or speaker on audio say the words below. Or ask a proficient English speaker to say them. In each word, underline the syllable with primary stress—the syllable that is longer and clearer.

Examples: suc-<u>ceed</u>, pes-si-<u>mis</u>-tic

1. ca-reer
2. your-self
3. a sur-vey
4. an ob-ject
5. to ob-ject
6. land-lord
7. e-co-no-my

8. e-co-no-mi-cal
9. re-sponse
10. re-spon-si-bil-i-ty
11. to se-par-ate
12. se-par-at-ed
13. of-fice
14. of-fi-cial

Check your answers with your teacher.

Note: Some longer words have secondary stress. The verb *to separate* has primary stress on the first syllable ("SE-") and secondary stress on the last syllable ("-ate"). Although syllables with secondary stress are not as strong as syllables with primary stress, syllables with secondary stress *do* have clear vowels.

Rules and Practices:
Using Parts of Speech to Predict Stress

It is always a good idea to learn the stress pattern of every new word. Some word groups, however, have predictable stress patterns. For example, it is useful to know that almost 90 percent of the two-syllable nouns in English (GARden, FREEdom, ANswer) have first-syllable stress. Here are some other helpful guidelines.

Rule 5-1

CD 2; Track 4

Listen to these compound nouns. Where is the primary stress?

deadline	meet the deadline
lifestyle	an active lifestyle
traffic jam	stuck in a traffic jam

✔ *Put the primary stress on the (first, last) noun in one-word and two-word compound nouns.*

> *Examples:* AIRport, LAPtop, HAMburger
> FAX machine, AIR conditioner, BASEball player

Rule 5-2

CD 2; Track 5

Listen to these compound adverbs of location. Where is the primary stress?

outdoors	works outdoors
southwest	from the southwest
downtown	went downtown

✔ *Put the primary stress on the (first, last) word of compound adverbs.*

> *Examples:* outSIDE, upSTAIRS, northWEST

Rule 5-3

CD 2; Track 6

Listen to these reflexive pronouns. Where is the stress?

myself	went by myself
themselves	finished it themselves

✔ *Stress -self or -selves.*

> *Example:* herSELF

Note this exception to Rule 5-1: If the second noun "is composed of" the material of the first noun, stress both nouns—SILK TIE, WOOL COAT, COTton SHIRT, CREAM CHEESE, PAper TOWELS, and APple PIE.

Exercise 1

Say the following compounds with the teacher or speaker on audio. Or take turns saying the words with a partner. The most important signal of stress is length, so stretch the stressed syllables out.

Suggestion: Add movement to your practice. Start with a closed fist. Open your fist as you say stressed syllables and close your fist on unstressed syllables.

Examples: V-O-I-C-E   mail

                 R-E-S-T   room

ONE-WORD COMPOUND NOUNS

Sunday	football	mailbox
background	bookstore	roommate
homework	bedroom	keyboard
lawsuit	newspaper	software

Other: _____

TWO-WORD COMPOUND NOUNS

car keys	post office	service charge
seat belt	parking deck	drug store
child care	lunch hour	rush hour
health care	Web site	gas station

Other: _____

COMPOUND ADVERBS

upstairs	underfoot	overseas
outside	southeast	uphill

Choose three compounds you use regularly. Write typical sentences you might say with them. Dictate your sentences to your partner.

a. _____

b. _____

c. _____

Exercise 2

Work with a partner.

Student A: Ask the question. Monitor your partner's answer for stress.
Student B: Close the book. Answer the question.

Examples: *Student A:* What do you call . . .   *Student B:*

. . . a pot for coffee?   a COFfee pot!

. . . the man who moves like a spider?   SPIder-Man!

1. a store that sells shoes   (SHOE store)
2. a pad for writing notes   (NOTEpad)
3. paper with news   (NEWSpaper)
4. a driver of a cab   (CAB driver)
5. a card with your name and business   (BUSiness card)
6. a school for the study of law   (LAW school)

(*Switch Roles*)

7. food service in a hotel room   (ROOM service)
8. a spoon for tea   (TEAspoon)
9. a book that tells you how to cook   (COOKbook)
10. a station that sells gas   (GAS station)
11. games on video   (VIDeo games)
12. a description of a job   (JOB description)

Rule 5-4

Compare the stress patterns of the phrases with two-noun compounds.

Phrases / Noun Compounds

FIVE DAYS / WEEK days

FREE CALL / PHONE call

✔ *In adjective + noun phrases, stress both words. In noun + noun compounds, put more stress on the first word.*

Example: SPARE KEYS / HOUSE keys

Exercise 3

With a partner, fill in each blank with the best choice from the box. Check your answers.

SUN	TEAM ✔	HAIR	POST
GOLF	PEN	COUGH	SOCcer

Phrases (2 stresses)	**Noun Compounds (1 stress)**
1. HARD WORK	_____TEAM_____ work
2. MAIN COURSE	_____ course
3. DARK GLASSes	_____ glasses
4. LARGE DRYer	_____ dryer
5. STRONG MEDicine	_____ medicine
6. NEW OFfice	_____ office
7. RUBber BALL	_____ ball

With your partner, take turns practicing the stress patterns in the phrases and the noun compounds.

Exercise 4

What is important when you look for a place to live? Select your top five criteria from the box below and write them on the next page.

ADJECTIVE + NOUN PHRASES				
LOW RENT	BIG ROOMS	FRESH PAINT	SAFE NEIGHborhood	QUIet BUILDing
NOUN COMPOUNDS				
BUS stop	BEDrooms	DISHwasher	AIR conditioner	WASHing machine
SIDEwalks	PLAYground	FIREplace	PARKing lot	seCURity gate

Examples: _____ safe neighborhood _____

_____ dishwasher _____

1. _____

2. _____

3. _____

4. _____

5. _____

Other: _____

Practice saying your choices. Then report your top two or three choices to a small group. Tell your group what is *least* important and why.

Rule 5-5

CD 2; Track 9

Listen to the stress in numbers like *50* and *15*. What is the stress pattern?

12:50 / 12:15

gate 40 / gate 14

bus 30 / bus 13

☑ **a.** *Stress the first syllable in ten numbers. Stress the -teen syllable when it is the last word in the phrase.*

Examples: It's twelve FIFty. / It's twelve fifTEEN.
Go to gate FORty. / Go to gate fourTEEN.

☑ **b.** *When the –teen number is in the middle of the phrase, usually stress both syllables.*

Examples: You need FIFty credits. / You need FIFTEEN credits.
That'll be THIRty dollars. / That'll be THIRTEEN dollars.

A Helpful Hint

Another way to recognize the difference between numbers like *forty* and *fourteen* is the pronunciation of the letter *t*. In *–teen* numbers *t* sounds like a clear /t/ — *gate fourTEEN*. In ten numbers, the *t* sounds like a quick /d/ sound: *gate FORdy, gate FIFdy,* and so on.

Exercise 5

With a partner, guess the correct answers.

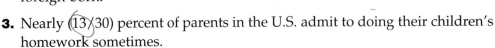

Then listen to your teacher or the speaker on audio say the sentences. Circle the numbers you hear.

CD 2; Track 10

1. Many people in the U.S. cannot wake up by themselves. About (19 / 90) percent depend on alarms.

2. In 2002, about (17 / 70) percent of Florida's population was foreign-born.

3. Nearly (13 / 30) percent of parents in the U.S. admit to doing their children's homework sometimes.

4. About (14 / 40) percent of the people in the U.S. have broken a bone.

5. In the U.S., about (15 / 50) percent of all Ph.D. engineering students are foreign-born.

6. Around (15 / 50) percent of Americans describe themselves as shy.

7. In 1980, 12 percent of doctors in the U.S. were women; in 2005, (13 / 30) percent were.

8. Friday, the (13th / 30th) is considered an unlucky date.

9. About (18 / 80) percent of North American men say they would marry the same woman again.

10. About (15 / 50) percent of all fatal two-car crashes are alcohol-related.

11. In 1970, (18 / 80) percent of college freshmen in the U.S. said their goal was to develop a meaningful philosophy of life.

12. In 2005, (17 / 70) percent of college freshmen in the U.S. said their goal was to be well-off financially.

Check your answers. Take turns practicing the sentences.

Rule 5-6

Listen to these two-syllable verbs with a prefix (*re–*, *con–*, *ad–*) and a base. Where is the stress?

CD 2; Track 11

require	require a reservation
convince	convince the voters
admit	I must admit

✔ *Stress the final syllable or base in most two-syllable verbs with a prefix.*

Examples: reCEIVE, deCIDE, preFER

Rule 5-7

CD 2; Track 12

English has a number of two-syllable verbs that are also used as nouns. What is the difference in stress?

Verb	Noun		Verb	Noun
conduct	conduct		produce	produce
desert	desert		permit	permit
record	record		present	present

✔ *Stress the second syllable in the verbs and the first syllable in the nouns.*

Examples:

Verb	Noun
conDUCT	CONduct
preSENT	PREsent

CD 2; Track 13

Listen to the verb-noun pairs above. Can you describe the vowel sound in the first syllable of the verbs? In the first syllable of the nouns?

Exercise 6

With your partner, say the words in each list.

Nouns	Verbs		Nouns	Verbs
net-work	en-joy		re-cord	re-cord
con-cepts	pre-fer		pro-gress	pro-gress
of-fice	com-pare		con-tracts	con-tracts
feed-back	as-sume		per-mit	per-mit
as-pects	a-chieve		sub-ject	sub-ject
in-come	ob-tained		in-ter-net	in-ter-fere
in-put	im-plied		o-ver-time	o-ver-sleep
fac-tor	as-sess		un-der-dog	un-der-stand

CD 2; Track 14

Listen to the teacher or speaker on audio say the words. Underline the stressed syllable in each word.

Now check at least five words you are likely to use. Say those words in a sentence.

Note: Some two-syllable noun-verb pairs do not shift stress (rePORT, rePLY, ANswer). See Appendix B for a list of noun-verb pairs *with* and *without* stress shift.

Rule 5-8

CD 2; Track 15

Listen to the stress pattern in two-word verbs. Which word has the stronger stress?

print out   Print it out.

put off   He put it off.

✔ *Give more stress to the second word or the particle.*

Examples: print OUT, look UP.

Note: Some two-word verbs have noun forms. Compare the stress patterns.

Nouns	Verbs
Here's the HANDout.	He handed it OUT.
Let's get TAKEout.	Let's take it OUT.
That's a RIPoff.	I got ripped OFF.

Exercise 7

Work with a partner.
Student A: Say word **a.** or **b.** Monitor Student B's response.
Student B: Say the matching sentence.

Example: *Student A:* obJECT
              Student B: Does anyone strongly *object*?

STUDENT A	STUDENT B
1. a. OBject	**a.** Money is no *object*.
b. obJECT	**b.** Does anyone strongly *object*?
2. a. PROduce	**a.** Garlic is in the *produce* section.
b. proDUCE	**b.** Robert Redford acts, *produces*, and directs.
3. a. WORKout	**a.** George begins every day with a *workout*.
b. work OUT	**b.** The job didn't *work out* the way I'd expected.
4. a. PRINTout	**a.** There are two examples on the *printout*.
b. print OUT	**b.** I didn't get a chance to *print it out*.
5. a. CONtract	**a.** They just signed a *contract* on a house.
b. conTRACT	**b.** How did she *contract* malaria?

(Switch Roles)

6. a. LOOKout	**a.** Be on the *lookout* for a parking spot.
b. look OUT	**b.** *Look out* for that car!
7. a. PREsent	**a.** How long have you been in your *present* job?
b. preSENT	**b.** After the speakers *present*, we can ask questions.
8. a. LAYoff	**a.** Sergio's worried about the *layoffs*.
b. lay OFF	**b.** He expects to be *laid off*.
9. a. PROject	**a.** Luba is directing the *project*.
b. proJECT	**b.** We didn't accurately *project* expenses.
10. a. CLEANup	**a.** The *cleanup* began immediately after the tsunami.
b. clean UP	**b.** A crew comes into the office every night to *clean up*.

Exercise 8

CD 2; Track 16

In pairs, take turns saying the words and sentences below. After you say each sentence, listen to your teacher or the speaker on audio say the same sentence. Were your stress patterns correct?

Example: (pay back)   I'll *pay* you *back* as soon as possible.

1. (paycheck)   Malik deposited his *paycheck*.

2. (newspaper)   I based that on what I read in the *newspaper*.

3. (overwhelmed)   Tai was *overwhelmed* by the responsibilities of his new job.

4. (outgrow)   It's just a phase. He'll *outgrow* it.

5. (dropouts)   Unemployment is high among high school *dropouts*.

6. (give up)   Don't *give up* so easily.

7. (convert, *verb*)   Can you *convert* Fahrenheit to Celsius?

8. (suspects, *noun*)   Have the police identified any *suspects*?

9. (runway, took off)   We sat next to the *runway* for hours before we *took off*.

10. (pick up, thirty)   I'll *pick* you *up* at seven-*thirty*.

11. (rejected)   They *rejected* our proposal.

12. (homework, explained, handout)   The *homework* is *explained* in the *handout*.

A Helpful Hint

When you use abbreviations, stress *each* letter or symbol. The last letter gets slightly more stress.

Examples: C D   (Compact Disk)

M A   (Master of Arts)

E U   (European Union)

When you say three or more stressed elements in sequence, slow your rate of speech.

Examples: H $_2$ O   (Water)

T G I F   (Thank Goodness It's Friday)

Y M C A   (Young Men's Christian Association)

Exercise 9

Part A: With a partner, write the abbreviations and symbols for the following:

1. _____ Los Angeles

2. _____ intelligence quotient

3. _____ World Health Organization

4. _____ carbon dioxide

5. _____ parental guidance

6. _____ automatic teller machine

7. _____ certified public accountant

8. _____ cardiopulmonary resuscitation

9. _____ digital video disk

10. _____ chief executive officer

CD 2; Track 17   Say each abbreviation above. Then listen to the speaker on audio say it. Or take turns saying the abbreviations with a partner. Monitor your partner.

Part B: What do these abbreviations mean?

11. GPA _Great Point Average_

12. VIP _____

13. HR _Human resorces_

14. PC _Politiquili correct_

15. HMO _____

16.

NEW YEAR CELEBRATION
Dec. 31
9:00
The NELSONS
R.S.V.P. REGRETS
270-3256

_____

17.

FYI
Here is a draft of the report.
Jim

_____

18.

Peggy,
Call home ASAP.
Bev

_____

Communicative Practice: No E-mail Fridays

To encourage more face-to-face communication, some offices have a "No E-mail Fridays" policy. On Fridays, employees deliver all messages to co-workers in person.

DIRECTIONS: Work with three people. Choose one speaker and two listeners. Imagine that it is a "No E-mail Friday."

Speaker: Give the information in the e-mail on the next page to your listeners. Do not read.

Listeners: Take notes on the important information. If you do not understand, ask the speaker to clarify. When the speaker is finished, compare your notes.

Preview the stress in these words and abbreviations:

BCBA	set UP	CONtact information
EVeryone	take DOWN	SIXty
OAKland	sign UP	outSIDE
COpy room	inCLUDE	SIGNup sheets
CELL number		

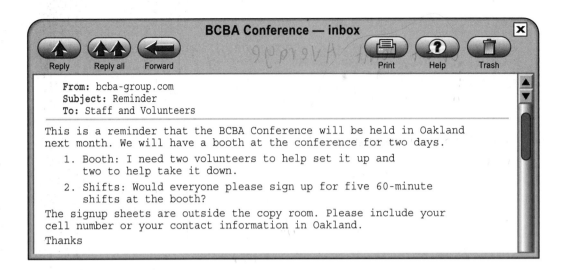

Prime-Time Practice

Oral Journal

Discuss your regular weekly household chores and activities.

Step 1: Preview stress patterns in key vocabulary below.

Sample Nouns: housework, weekends, weekdays, bedroom, bathroom, phone calls, grocery store, drug store, dish detergent, toothpaste, ATM

Sample Verbs: get together, clean up, stop in, put away, hang up, throw away, take out, catch up, drop off, work out, pick up, call up, eat out

Step 2: Record yourself discussing the following questions. Do not exceed one minute. What regular household chores do you have to do? What errands do you have to run? What items do you have to pick up? Which tasks do you especially like or dislike and why?

Sample sentence: On <u>WEEK</u>ends, I like to <u>get toGETHer</u> with friends, but usually I have to <u>catch UP</u> on <u>HOME</u>work.

Step 3: Listen to your recording. Note stress patterns in nouns and verbs. Write the words with stress patterns you want to improve.

NOUNS	VERBS
_____	_____
_____	_____
_____	_____

Step 4: Record your response again. Listen, and submit the recording to your teacher for feedback.

"Oral Review: Stress in Words" appears at the end of Chapter 6.

Stress in Longer Words

In Chapter 5, you used parts of speech to predict stress in words. Another way to predict stress is with suffixes or word endings. Some suffixes, like *-ment*, *-able*, and *-er* do *not* affect word stress.

> a-CHIEVE
> a-CHIEVE - ment
> a-CHIEV - a - ble
> a-CHIEV - er

Other suffixes, like *-ic*, *-ity*, and *-ion do* affect word stress.

> HIS - tor - y
> his - TOR - ic

> MA - jor
> ma - JOR - i - ty

> DE - mon - strate
> de - mon - STRA - tion

Listen to your teacher say each set of words below. Can you hear a regular pattern of stress in each set?

1. trainee	referee	guarantee	absentee
2. historic	specific	democratic	chaotic
3. majority	ability	facility	priority

Now say the words *with* your teacher.

1. traiNEE	refeREE	guaranTEE	absenTEE
2. hisTORic	speCIFic	demoCRATic	chaOTic Kaio
3. maJORity	aBILity	faCILity	priORity

In this chapter, you will learn guidelines for suffixes that affect word stress. These guidelines will help you pronounce words more clearly, especially long academic, scientific, and technical words that come from Latin and Greek.

Sillaby before

Listen!

monday

CD 2; Track 18
CD 2; Track 19

Listening Activity 1

Listen to your teacher or the speaker on audio read the passage two times. The first time, close your book and listen for meaning. The second time, open your books and write the missing words in the blanks.

SPACE STATIONS

When the United States and Russia decided to __cooperate__ on

Mir

the new International Space Station (ISS), the United States began sending

astronauts to live on the Russian space station *Mir*. Experiments on *Mir* provided

Ai

valuable data for the __operation__ of the ISS. The most valuable

lessons, however, were learned through daily life on *Mir*.

Mir was not like the comfortable spaceships in movies. It was small,

desorganization

crowded, and __choatic__. The main section was a narrow tube

filled with __electronics__ and crew members living in zero

__gravity__. The crew members wore the same clothes for two weeks.

They had to recycle sweat for drinking water. Power problems forced them to

spend time in the dark. Problems with the cooling system caused the

ge

__humnidity__ to rise and temperatures to reach 95 degrees Fahrenheit.

__comunication__ problems resulted in their __inability__ to

get regular e-mail messages.

All in all, *Mir* provided useful training for the ISS. Officials now realize that crew

members need both __technical__ training and the ability to

uncomfortable

__tolarate__ difficult living conditions. Despite the hardships, a private

company called Space Adventures has been taking __reservations__ for

tourist trips to the ISS!

Check your answers with your teacher.

Listening Activity 2

Compare the underlined vowels in these word pairs.

A	B
1. b<u>a</u>nd	HUSb<u>a</u>nd
2. m<u>a</u>n	WOm<u>a</u>n
3. sp<u>a</u>	sp<u>a</u>GHEtti
4. <u>a</u>d	<u>a</u>dVICE
5. t<u>a</u>ble	VEGet<u>a</u>ble

In which column were the vowels clear and strong? In which column were the vowels weak and unclear? Unstressed syllables often have the weak schwa vowel sound /ə/, as in *about* or *us*.

Listening Activity 3

Listen to the teacher or the speaker on audio say each word twice. Each time you hear /ə/, put a line through the vowel.

Examples: METH - ø̸d

bi - ø̸ - LOG - i̸ - ca̸l

1. spe - CI - fic	**7.** OR - e - gon
2. de - VE - lop	**8.** EX - cel - lent
3. an -NOUNCE - ment	**9.** DE - mon - strate
4. con - CLU - sion	**10.** PRE - si - dent
5. pro - FES - sion - al	**11.** CA - len - dar
6. OR - gan	**12.** SPE - ci - fy

Check your answers with your teacher or in your dictionary. How many different spellings can the schwa sound have? _____

Note: Most unstressed vowels sound like /ə/, but sometimes they sound like /ɪ/ as in *hit*.

Rules and Practices:
Using Suffixes to Predict Stress in Longer Words

Rule 6-1

🎧
CD 2; Track 22

Listen to the words that end with these suffixes. Can you identify a stress pattern that applies to all of the suffixes below?

a. -ion *the syllaby before the word*
location
condition
definition

c. -ity
security
minority
liability

e. -ify
justify
∧ identify
specify

g. -ial
financial
official
initial

b. -ic
chaotic
academic
economic

d. -ical
practical
technical
economical

f. -ian
musician
physician
electrician

h. -ious
religious
ambitious
delicious

✔ *Stress the syllable immediately before these suffixes that begin with the letter i.*

Examples:

a. seLECT**ion**

b. scienTIF**ic**

c. possiBIL**ity**

d. hisTOR**ical**

e. CLAR**ify**

f. poliTIC**ian***

g. poTENT**ial**

h. susPIC**ious****

The most important stress-shifting suffixes are included in Rule 6-1: *-ion, -ic, -ity,* and *-(ic)al*. They account for about 90 percent of all shifts in word stress.

1. The -ian suffix is one syllable when preceded by c, t, g, and s, as in mu-si-cian**; it is two syllables when preceded by b, d, r, and other consonants, as in Ca-na-**di-an** and li-bra-**ri-an**.*

***2. The -ious suffix is one syllable when preceded by c, t, and g, as in sus-PI-**cious** and re-LI-**gious**; it is two syllables when preceded by r, n, and other consonants, as in mys-TE-**ri-ous** and PRE-**vi-ous**.*

Exercise 1

With a partner, write the words below in the correct column based on the stress pattern.

majority	authority	technical	estimation
chemical	economic	permission	reality
conclusion	creation	application	critical

poSITion	priORity	demoCRATic	PRACtical
Permission	majority	economic	technical
Conclusion	Authority	___	critical
Stimation	reality	___	chemical
Creation			
Application			

Check your answers.

CD 2; Track 23 Now repeat the words in each column in Exercise 1 after your teacher or the speaker on audio. Stretch a rubber band on the stressed syllable of each word.

po – SI – tion

Rule 6-2

CD 2; Track 24 Listen to the word groups with these suffixes. What is the stress pattern?

a. -graphy

biography

geography

bibliography

b. -logy

ecology

technology

radiology

✔ *Stress the syllable immediately before these suffixes.*

Examples: **a.** phoTOgraphy **b.** pharmaCOlogy

Rule 6-3

CD 2; Track 25 Listen to the words with suffixes like *-ee, -eer, -ese, -ette, -esque,* and *-ique.* What is the stress pattern?

engineer a chemical engineer

technique a new technique

Japanese written in Japanese

✔ *Stress falls on these suffixes.*

Examples: carEER, unIQUE, ChinESE

Note: These are exceptions to Rules 6-1 to 6-3: 1. *-ic:* POlitics, RHEtoric, CAtholic; 2. *-ee:* comMITtee, COFfee; 3. *-ion:* TElevision.

Exercise 2

Fill in the blanks by adding suffixes *-ion*, *-ic*, *-ical*, *-ity*, *-ify*, *-ian*, *-logy*, or *-ese* to the base words. Underline the syllable (or vowel) in each word with the primary stress.

Base Word	Noun	Verb	Adjective
Examples: real	reality	realize	realistic
economy	economy economics	economize	economic economical
1. specify	specification	specify	*Specific*
2. major	*majority*	X	major
3. method	methodology	X	*Methodical*
4. person	personality	*personilize*	personal
5. photograph	*photography*	photograph	photographic
6. Japan	Japanese	X	*Japanesse*
7. individual	*Individuallyti*	X	individualistic
8. philosophy	philosopher	philosophize	*Philosotxal*
9. mechanism	*mechanic*	mechanize	mechanical
10. electric	*electricity*	electrify	electrical electronic

Compare your answers with those of other class members.

 Say the words with the speaker on audio or take turns saying the words with a partner.
CD 2; Track 26 Nod your head slightly as you say the stressed syllables.

A Helpful Hint for the TOEFL iBT®

When you listen to the lectures in the Integrated Speaking Tasks, make a note of the stress patterns in key terms that you are likely to use in your oral response.

Rule 6-4

 Listen to these verbs ending in *-ate*. About 1,000 of these verbs exist in English, and
CD 2; Track 27 they are common in academic and business settings. Can you identify a stress pattern?

demonstrate	easy to demonstrate
communicate	need to communicate
participate	refused to participate

✔ *Stress falls two syllables before the -ate suffix in North American English.*

Examples: GE - ner - ate
ES - tim - ate
ne - GO - ti - ate

The second syllable before the *-ate* suffix is stressed even if *-ed* or *-ing* is added. The stress shifts when the *-ion* suffix is added. With practice, the pattern will become automatic.

col - LA - bor - ate
col - LA - bo - rat - ed
col - LA - bo - rat - ing
col - la - bo - RA - tion

enTYmology
InSects

Note: See Appendix C for a more complete list of suffixes that affect word stress.

"Norman won't collaborate."

Exercise 3

CD 2; Track 28 Say these words with the teacher or the speakers on audio. Snap your fingers on the stressed syllables.

INdicate	INdicated	INdicating	(indiCAtion)
DEmonstrate	DEmonstrated	DEmonstrating	(demonSTRAtion)
CONcentrate	CONcentrated	CONcentrating	(concenTRAtion)
inVEStigate	inVEStigated	inVEStigating	(investiGAtion)
parTIcipate	parTIcipated	parTIcipating	(particiPAtion)

Did you notice that in *-ate* verbs, the *-ate* syllable has secondary stress? The vowel is clear, and the *-ate* syllable sounds like the word *ate*.

A Helpful Hint

Some *-ate* words are adjectives, nouns, and adverbs as well as verbs.

Noun: Miriam's applying to **graduate** school in psychology.

Adjective: The service at that restaurant is just **adequate**.

Adverb: I haven't seen Ann for 10 years, but I recognized her **immediately**.

In *-ate* adjectives, nouns, and adverbs, the primary stress is the same, but the *-ate* syllable is usually unstressed. It sounds like /ɪt/ or the word *it*.

NOUN/ADJECTIVE	VERB
That's a completely **SEparate** issue. (-ate = *it*)	Let's try to **SEparate** the issues. (-ate = *ate*)
Can you give us an **EStimate**? (-ate = *it*)	Can you **EStimate** the cost? (-ate = *ate*)

Exercise 4

CD 2; Track 29

With a partner, take turns saying the words in the chart. Have your partner monitor you. Or check your pronunciation with the speaker on audio. Lengthen the stressed syllables.

Verb	GRAduate	apPROXimate	estimate	separate	duplicate
Add **-ed**	GRAduated	apPROXimated	estimated	separated	duplicated
Add **-ing**	GRAduating	apPROXimating	estimating	separating	duplicating
Noun or Adj.	GRAduate = *it*	apPROXimate = *it*	estimate	separate	duplicate
Add **-ion**	graduAtion	approxiMAtion	estimation	separation	duplication

Now say the words chorally with your class.

Exercise 5

Work with a partner. Apply what you know about stress and say the words and phrases below.

Example: baseball players – terminated   – contracts

           BASEball players – TERminated – CONtracts

1. roommate – graduate student – sociology

2. post office – locate – Peachtree Street

3. remove – laptop computers – airport security

4. mechanic – gave – estimate (*n.*)

5. celebrate – birthday – June 15

6. organic farmers – harmful chemicals – produce (*n.*)

7. Who – Democratic candidate

8. how – improve – economic status

Now take turns making sentences with the words above. Monitor your partner's stress patterns. Remember *-s* and *-ed* endings.

Example: baseball players – terminated – contracts

The two best baseball players on the team terminated their contracts.

Communicative Practice: Library Orientation

InfoGap

With widespread access to the Internet, fewer people use libraries. *Student A,* however, wants to keep libraries healthy and has a floor map to the town library on page 209. *Student B* has the "Key to Location" of the areas of the library below.

Student A: Look at the list below your map. Report six to eight areas of greatest interest and why you are interested in those areas.

Student B: Circle those areas on the Key below. Then tell *Student A* the floor and letter of each area.

Student A: Write each area of interest in the blank on your map.

Student B: Key to Location

First Floor	Second Floor	Third Floor
A. Circulation (checkout)	**F.** Media/CDs/DVDs	**L.** Education
B. Current periodicals/Foreign language newspapers	**G.** Photography Gallery	**M.** Anthropology
	H. Copy Services	**N.** Political Science
C. Rest Rooms	**I.** Psychology	**O.** Cookbooks
D. Fire Exit	**J.** Economics	**P.** Mathematics
E. Workstations/Databases	**K.** Biological Sciences	**Q.** Engineering

Prime-Time Practice

Sharing Information about a Conference
Use what you have learned about word stress to pronounce long, difficult words you might not have said before.

Step 1: Underline and practice the primary stress in each boldfaced word. If necessary, check your dictionary.

Step 2: Imagine you are on the phone with a friend who might be interested in this conference. You want to persuade your friend to attend with you. Tell your friend about the conference, and record your explanation.

Usability Professionals Association (UPA) announces a conference on . . .

DESIGNING NEW **PRODUCTS** AND **TECHNOLOGY**
November **14**

1:30	**Keynote:** Dr. Paul Wood, **pioneer** in human-computer interaction "Information **Security** vs. **Usability** and **Simplicity**"
2:30	**Workshops** (open to all **attendees**) **1. Conducting Usability** Testing with Older Adults **2.** Web **Accessibility** for People with **Disabilities** **3. Democratic Elections** and **Electronic** Voting Machines **4. Software Engineering** and **Navigation** of **Web** sites
5:30	**Reception – Ballroom**

For more **information: www.wudsac.sdu.edu**

Step 3: Listen to your recording. Monitor your pronunciation of the boldfaced words.

I was satisfied with these stress patterns:	I was *not* satisfied with these stress patterns:
1. _____	1. _____
2. _____	2. _____
3. _____	3. _____
4. _____	4. _____
5. _____	5. _____

Make changes and corrections at the end of the recording.

Extend Your Skills . . . to a Small-Group Discussion

Your task is to select a city for the next Summer Olympic Games. Work in committees of three to five.

First, preview the stress patterns in these key terms:

AIRport	STREET crime
AIRlines	huMIDity
BASEball	HANDball
WEIGHTlifting	QUALity
uNIQUE	faCILities
TAble tennis	staBILity
poLICE force	FOREcast
gymNASTics	CORporate
accessiBILity	MEDical
accommoDAtions	VOLleyball
transporTAtion	hospiTALity
aQUATics	FREEways
FOOTball	

Each person should select his or her favorite city in the world to host the next Summer Games. Write your choice and the choices of the other committee members in the chart on the next page.

Now evaluate your city using a scale from 1 to 5.

5 = excellent 4 = good 3 = average 2 = fair 1 = poor		*(name of city)*	*(name of city)*	*(name of city)*	*(name of city)*	*(name of city)*

CATEGORIES AND COMMENTS	YOUR CITY	1	2	3	4
Accessibility — Airport/airlines:					
Accommodations — Number/quality of hotel rooms:					
Transportation — Freeways/subways/taxicabs:					
Entertainment — Restaurants/nightlife/attractions:					
For aquatics, baseball, basketball, volleyball, table tennis, sailing, weightlifting, gymnastics, etc.:					
Languages — Number spoken:					
Political Stability of Country:					
Security — Street crime/police force:					
Weather — July forecast/humidity:					
Other — Corporate support/hospitality/medical facilities/other unique aspects of the city:					
TOTAL SCORES					

Add up total points (maximum score is 50). Discuss your ratings and reach agreement on the one best candidate.

Summarize your group's choice on the following Outline for Bid. Select one or more group members to present your bid to the class in two minutes or less.

Make your organization clear with transitions such as *one positive point, next,* and *in addition.* See the Outline for a list of other useful transitions.

To make your bid interesting, be sure to provide specific examples. For example, if your city received a rating of **excellent** in the category *Languages,* specify the languages spoken in that city.

In your summary, indicate that you have *fully* considered your choice by mentioning one weak area. Finish your summary, however, with another mention of the one or two greatest strengths; your listeners will remember what they hear last.

After the groups present their bids, the class can select the most convincing presentation.

OUTLINE FOR BID

Useful Phrases

We'd like to nominate . . .	Top candidate: _____ Points: _____
Our candidate for . . .	
	Strengths:
First . . .	**1.**
Next . . .	**2.**
In addition . . .	**3.**
Another positive aspect . . .	**4.**
The greatest strength . . .	**5.**
Finally . . .	
In summary . . .	Summary:
In conclusion . . .	**1.** One weakness:
In closing . . .	**2.** Two greatest strengths:

Oral Review: Stress in Words

Name: _____ Date: _____

Schedule an individual consultation with your teacher or submit the review on audio.

Part A: Circle the primary stress in each boldfaced word. Record the dialogs.

1. **A:** That was a great evening.

   B: It was! Remind me to call and thank them for their **hospitality**.

2. **A:** Their **medical** bills have been unbelievable.

   B: I know. **Unfortunately**, they can't get good **health insurance**.

3. **A:** Are you ready to order?

   B: Yeah. I'd like a **cheeseburger** and a **strawberry milkshake**.

4. **A:** Do you think we should **help** him **out**?

   B: I don't know. I think he can probably **figure** it **out** by **himself**.

5. **A:** What's wrong?

   B: I can't find my **homework**. I thought I put it in my **backpack**.

6. **A:** Excuse me. Why was my car towed? *toad, (toud), toed*

   B: Sorry. You're not **permitted** to park here without a **permit**. *noun*

7. **A:** Can you believe that? We're all getting a **paycut**.

   B: Yeah. Even though we all deserve a **substantial** raise. *substanial*

8. **A:** I heard that Jan is working on a **degree** in **pharmacology**.

   B: Yeah. I heard that too. I guess she **gave up** on **biology**.

Listen to your tape and underline the syllables you stressed. Did you stress the correct syllables? Were your stressed syllables longer and clearer than your unstressed syllables? Make corrections at the end of your recording.

Part B: Record yourself reading the passage "Space Stations" in Listening Activity 1. Listen to the recording. Monitor for word stress in the underlined words. Make corrections at the end of the recording.

BEYOND THE PRONUNCIATION CLASSROOM

Applying for a Library Card

Now that you are becoming more comfortable with new pronunciation patterns, each chapter will end with *Beyond the Pronunciation Classroom*. In this section, you will practice pronunciation points in everyday interactions.

Pronunciation Point: Stress patterns in words.

Task: Go to the public library and apply for a library card.

- Take necessary I.D. (driver's license, checkbook, or utility bill).

- Find out the lending period for various items (books, books on CD, and DVDs?).

- Ask about the fine for overdue materials (15 cents/30 cents/50 cents a day?).

Before: With your class, anticipate the interaction. Preview the stress patterns in key words and rehearse with your partner.

KEY VOCABULARY	STRESS PATTERN
library card	_____
I.D. or identification	_____
checkbook	_____
utility bill	_____
driver's license	_____
CD	_____
DVD	_____
fifteen cents / fifty cents	_____

After: Discuss your experience with your class.

Midcourse Self-Evaluation

Part A: Circle the answers.   (1 = not at all . . . 5 = very much)

1. My general awareness of English
   speech patterns has improved.   1   2   3   4   5

2. I have a better idea of why I am
   sometimes not understood.   1   2   3   4   5

3. I am beginning to hear problems
   in my own speech.   1   2   3   4   5

4. My speech is beginning to improve.   1   2   3   4   5

5. I want to improve my intelligibility. 1   2   3   4   5

6. I have worked hard to improve
   my intelligibility.   1   2   3   4   5

Part B: In an AUDIO JOURNAL, answer these questions.

1. In what ways has my speech improved?

2. What are three areas in which I want my speech to improve before the end
   of the course?

   a. _____

   b. _____

   c. _____

3. What will I have to do to achieve these changes?

4. What is one speaking situation in which I want my speech to improve?

Rhythm in Phrases and Sentences

Every language has its own rhythm or beat. Two different rhythm patterns are represented in the pictures below.

These vehicles are the same size. They are the same distance apart. They are moving at the same speed. If you were waiting to cross this busy street, what kind of a sound pattern would you hear as the cars moved past?

▲ In some languages, every syllable has more or less equal emphasis.

The vehicles below are different sizes and lengths. If you were waiting to cross this busy street, what kind of a sound pattern would you hear?

▲ In other languages, some words and syllables are strong and others are weak.

Which figure is more like the rhythm pattern of your language? Which figure is more like the rhythm of English?

In Chapters 5 and 6, you learned about stressed and unstressed syllables in words. In this chapter, you will learn about stressed and unstressed words and syllables in phrases and sentences. This combination of strong and weak beats creates the **rhythm** of English.

Something to Think About

When speakers of American English are irritated or determined, they sometimes give full, equal stress to every word and syllable.

Examples: I HAVE HAD E-NOUGH.
THIS MUST BE DONE BY NOON.

If you stress every word and syllable equally, you might sound abrupt, angry, or impatient without intending to.

Listen!

Listening Activity 1

Just as words have stressed and unstressed syllables, so do phrases and sentences.

CD 2; Track 30

Listen to your teacher or the speaker on audio say these pairs. In each pair, the rhythm pattern of the word is repeated in the phrase.

Example: re JECT ed   He WRECKED it.

WORD	PHRASE
1. engineer	He can hear.
2. quantity	Talk to me.
3. yourself	The shelf.
4. convert (verb)	She's hurt.
5. presented	He sent it.
6. progressed	The best.
7. permit (noun)	Learn it.
8. conclusion	The blue one.

If you did not hear the rhythm, replay the audio and listen with your eyes closed.

Listening Activity 2

CD 2; Track 31

Each phrase has a *different* number of syllables but takes the *same* length of time to say. Listen to your teacher or the speaker on audio say the phrases.

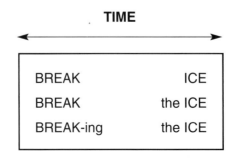

```
GIVE              WAY
GIVE              a-WAY
GIV-ing           a-WAY
GIV-ing it        a-WAY
```

```
QUICK             CALL
QUICK             re-CALL
QUICK-ly          re-CALL
```

Which syllables were longer and stronger? Which syllables were shorter and weaker?

CD 2; Track 32

Now say the phrases with your teacher or the speaker on audio. Tap the two strong beats in each phrase with the speaker. Say the stressed syllables *on* the beats. Fit the unstressed syllables *between* the beats.

Listening Activity 3

CD 2; Track 33

Poems and rhymes are one way to acquire rhythm patterns. Listen to your teacher or the speaker on audio say each of these popular rhymes for children two times. Write the number of strong beats in each line.

The House that Jack Built	Strong Beats
THIS is the HOUSE	2
that JACK BUILT	2
This is the malt	___
that lay in the house	___
that Jack built	___
This is the rat	___
that ate the malt	___
that lay in the house	___
that Jack built	___
This is the cat	___
that killed the rat	___
that ate the malt	___
that lay in the house	___
that Jack built.	___

Three Blind Mice	**Strong Beats**
Three blind mice!	3
See how they run!	___
They all ran after the farmer's wife,	___
She cut off their tails with a carving knife.	___
Have you ever seen such a sight in your life	___
As three blind mice?	___

Listening Activity 4

CD 2; Track 34

Part A: Listen to the dialog. Half of the words are missing.

CUSTOMER: Is it _____ to _change_ my _____ to _____ from _____ to _____?

AGENT: Uhh, _____, there are _____ _____ on the _____ _____ on _____.

CUSTOMER: _____ the _____ to _____ the _____?

AGENT: The _____ _____ with the _____ _____ is _____ _____. Do you _____ to _____ the _____?

Can you guess what the dialog is about?

CD 2; Track 35

Part B: Listen to the same conversation with the other half of the words missing.

CUSTOMER: _____ _____ possible _____ change _____ reservation _____ Los Angeles _____ Saturday _____ Sunday?

AGENT: _____ yes, _____ _____ two seats _____ _____ 9:30 flight _____ Sunday.

CUSTOMER: What's _____ cost _____ change _____ ticket?

AGENT: _____ total cost _____ _____ change fee _____ 300 dollars. _____ _____ want _____ change _____ reservation?

Now can you guess what the dialog is about?

CD 2; Track 36

Part C: Now listen to the complete dialog. Notice the stressed (highlighted) parts and the unstressed (shaded) parts.

CUSTOMER: Is it POSsible to CHANGE my reserVAtion to Los ANgeles from SAturday to SUNday?

AGENT: Uhh, YES, there are TWO SEATS on the 9:30 FLIGHT on SUNday.

CUSTOMER: WHAT'S the COST to CHANGE my TICKet?

AGENT: The TOtal COST with the CHANGE FEE is 300 DOLLars. Do you WANT to CHANGE the reserVAtion?

What kinds of words are strong and stressed in the dialog?

What kinds of words are weak or unstressed in the dialog?

Prime-Time Practice

Listen to proficient speakers of English on television. Pay attention to how they speak. Write your answers to these questions:

1. Listen to rhythm patterns in a news broadcast. Do you hear strong beats and weak beats? _____

2. Do you hear any weak, unstressed words? Can you identify some of these words and describe what they sound like?

   Example: __are__ *sounds like* __er__

   _____   _____

   _____   _____

   _____   _____

3. How important are the weak parts of the message for understanding?

   _____

4. Watch a few minutes of a TV drama or sitcom *without* the sound. Notice body movement, especially upper body movements of the arms, head, and eyes.

5. Turn the sound back on. What is the connection between upper body movement and the stressed parts of the message?

   _____

Discuss your answers with your teacher and other class members.

Rules and Practices: Stressed and Reduced Words

Listeners of English expect more important words to be strong and less important words to be weak. The strong words are the ones listeners pay the most attention to. Contrasting strong and weak words is a basic part of speaking clearly.

Rule 7-1

 Stress important content words.

NOUNS	MAIN VERBS	ADJECTIVES	ADVERBS
QUIZ	atTEND	LONG	QUITE
PAINT	TOUCH	CAREful	REALly

NEGATIVES	WH-WORDS	INTERJECTIONS
CAN'T	WHAT	YES
NOT	HOW	WOW

Content words carry most of the information.

Example: Be CAREful NOT to SIT on the WET PAINT.

Note: In content words of more than one syllable, like *CAREful,* stress the correct syllable.

Rule 7-2

 Reduce or weaken function words.

ARTICLES	CONJUNCTIONS	PREPOSITIONS	PRONOUNS	AUXILIARY VERBS
a	and	to	him	can
the	or	of	you	does

Function words make the grammar correct, but they do not carry as much information as content words.

Example: WHY does she DRIVE such a BIG CAR?

How do we reduce function words? Here are some ways:

a. Contractions: JOHN <u>is</u> an OLD FRIEND. → JOHN/z/ an OLD FRIEND.

b. Reduced Vowels   <u>Can you</u> SEE?   → /kən yə/ SEE?

c. Omitted Consonants: LET <u>him</u> GO.   → LET /əm/ GO.

Exercise 1

With a partner, work out the rhythmic pattern of each sentence. Circle the content words (or the stressed syllables of the content words).

CD 2; Track 37

Then say the sentences with the speaker on audio or practice with a partner as follows:

Student A: Say each sentence.

Student B: Write the number of strong beats you hear.

STUDENT A	STUDENT B
Example: I can't understand a thing.	3
1. I can completely understand.	_____
2. He wants to leave on time.	_____
3. It demonstrates his flexibility.	_____
4. It's not my first priority.	_____
5. He said he'd finish it as soon as possible.	_____

(Switch Roles)

6. Sorry I'm late.	_____
7. I'd like you to meet my sister.	_____
8. We'll see you on Monday or Tuesday.	_____
9. Her background is in mathematics.	_____
10. Most of the students are from China and India.	_____

Follow-up: Say the sentences *with* your partner.

Exercise 2

CD 2; Track 38

Say these rhymes and sentences *with* your teacher or the speaker on audio. The rhythm of each rhyme is repeated in the sentences that follow it.

Rhyme A: THREE BLIND MICE
            (Please sit down.)
            (Come back soon.)
            (Juan can't go.)
            (Don't get lost.)

            SEE HOW they RUN.
            (Lee went by bus.)
            (John found the disk.)
            (Tell Lin I called.)
            (That meal was great.)

Rhyme B: $\overline{\text{HICK}}$ory $\overline{\text{DICK}}$ory $\overline{\text{DOCK}}$
(Everyone's welcome to come.)
(Jan is the person to call.)
(Fix her a burger with cheese.)

The $\overline{\text{MOUSE}}$ ran $\overline{\text{UP}}$ the $\overline{\text{CLOCK}}$.
(I need to get some cash.)
(He wants to buy a car.)
(I'll have her call you back.)

Rhyme C: $\overline{\text{TWIN}}$kle, $\overline{\text{TWIN}}$kle $\overline{\text{LIT}}$tle $\overline{\text{STAR}}$,
(Let me help you pay the fee.)
(Don't forget the eggs and milk.)
(Tell me why you don't agree.)

$\overline{\text{HOW}}$ I $\overline{\text{WON}}$der $\overline{\text{WHAT}}$ you $\overline{\text{ARE}}$.
(Don't forget to leave a tip.)
(Thanks a lot for all you did.)
(Find a space and park your car.)

Did you notice that you had to shorten unstressed words and syllables to maintain the rhythm?

Exercise 3

CD 2; Track 39 With your teacher or the speakers on audio, step on the strong beats — just as Dorothy, the Scarecrow, and the Tin Man did in the *The Wizard of Oz.*

| LIons and | TIgers and | BEARS | oh MY |
| LIons and | TIgers and | BEARS | oh MY |

These words are longer, but the time between the strong beats is the same.

1	2	3	4
ELephants and	CObras and	CROcodiles	oh MY
ELephants and	CObras and	CROcodiles	oh MY

Now try these lists. Keep the same beat regardless of the number of syllables.

	1	2	3	4
Miseries:	SCHEdules and	comPUters and	HOMEwork	oh MY (2×)
Pleasures:	SPRINGtime and	vaCATions and	CHOcolate	oh MY (2×)
Courses:	CHEmistry and	ecoNOmics and	biOlogy	oh MY (2×)
Occupations:	engiNEERS and	meCHAnics and	DENtists	oh MY (2×)

Fill in each blank with one word. Practice with your partner.

	1	2	3	4
Miseries:	_____ and	_____ and	_____	oh MY
Pleasures:	_____ and	_____ and	_____	oh MY
Other _____ :	_____ and	_____ and	_____	oh MY

A Helpful Hint

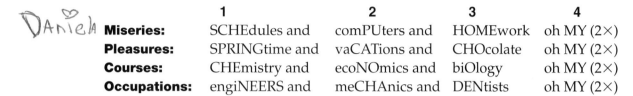

Changing your pronunciation, especially stress and rhythm, involves changes in breathing, facial expression, and movement. As a result, when you speak English, you might feel less Korean, Chinese, Russian, Vietnamese, Mexican, Brazilian, Thai, Afghani, or Nigerian. In other words, you may feel less like yourself.

Try to overcome resistance to pronunciation change because resistance can limit your progress. These suggestions might help:

1. View English pronunciation like a jacket that you can put on and take off, depending on who your listener is.

2. When you practice, think of a proficient English speaker you admire. Imitate his or her pronunciation, gestures, and expressions.

3. Remember that you can have speech that is accented AND clear. You need to be concerned only with English pronunciation features that cause misunderstanding and distraction.

Exercise 4

Say the following phrases with your teacher or the speaker on audio.

Phrase **a** is like a headline. It has only the important content words. Phrases **b**, **c**, and **d** have extra function words but have the same rhythm and take the *same* amount of time to say. Tap your pencil in time with the rhythm.

SAME TIME FOR EACH PHRASE

← →

TAP	*TAP*	*TAP*
1. a. SHARK	SCARES	MAN.
b. SHARK	SCARES	the MAN.
c. The SHARK is	SCARing	the MAN.
d. The SHARK has been SCARing the MAN.		

← →

TAP	*TAP*	*TAP*
2. a. SNOW	exPECted	FRIday.
b. SNOW is	exPECted	FRIday.
c. SNOW is	exPECted on	FRIday.
d. The SNOW is	exPECted on	FRIday.

← →

TAP	*TAP*	*TAP*
3. a. reTURN	BOOKS	MONday.
b. reTURN	BOOKS on	MONday.
c. reTURN the	BOOKS on	MONday.
d. You can reTURN the BOOKS on MONday.		

Exercise 5

Make each sentence passive. With your partner or with the speaker on audio, say both the active and passive sentences with the *same rhythm pattern*.

SAME TIME FOR EACH SENTENCE

← →

TAP	*TAP*	*TAP*
1. SPIELberg	diRECted	*E.T.*
E.T.	was directed	by Spielberg.

2. GATES   FOUNDed   MIcrosoft.

---

3. APple   introDUCED   the Ipod.

---

4. BELL   inVENTed   the TELephone.

---

5. The BEAtles   reCORDed   "YESterday."

Prime-Time Practice

What makes you feel good inside? Work out the rhythm patterns of these "natural highs" below. Record them and add three of your own.

• Falling in love • Seeing a good movie • Scoring a winning goal •
Finishing a good book • Walking on the beach • Getting a surprise visit •
Seeing a falling star • Getting an A plus • Solving a difficult problem •
Watching a beautiful sunset • Finishing a big project • Catching a fish

• _____

• _____

• _____

Listen to your tape and monitor the rhythm patterns. Re-record phrases you are not satisfied with.

Function Words

In the box on the next page are common one-syllable function words and their reduced pronunciations. These reductions are *not* poor English. They are a part of normal, everyday speech.

If you stress these words, your speech will be hard to understand. If you reduce these words, important information will stand out and your speech will be easier to understand. Notice how many of these function words have *schwa* /ə/.

	Pronunciation	Examples
Articles		
a	/ə/	a mistake
the	/ðə/	on the desk
an	/ən/	an emergency
Conjunctions		
or	/ər/	pass or fail
and	/ən/ or /n/	hot and humid
Prepositions		
of	/əv/	out of eggs
	/ə/	date of birth
to	/tə/	gone to lunch
for	/fər/	call for Paul
at	/ət/	at home
Pronouns		
him	/əm/ or /ɪm/	tell him
her	/ər/	introduce her
them	/əm/	call them
you	/yə/	Are you tired?
Auxiliary Verbs		
do	/də/	What do you want?
can	/kən/ or /kn/	Can you go?
have	/əv/ or /ə/	should have gone

Note these exceptions: Speakers stress function words in these contexts:

1. X: He's not sick. Y: YES, he <u>IS</u> SICK. (for special emphasis)
2. X: He CAN'T SWIM, <u>CAN</u> he? (in tag questions)
   Y: Yes, he <u>CAN</u>. (as the last word in the sentence).

You will learn more about context and stress in the following chapters.

Exercise 6

CD 2; Track 42

Listen and fill in the blanks with the function words you hear. (*Hint:* One of the missing words in each sentence is a pronoun or auxiliary verb with a disappearing *h:* ⱨim, ⱨer, ⱨis, ⱨe, ⱨas, or ⱨave.)

Example: __Did__ __he__ get the promotion?

1. The interviewer asked _____ some questions.

2. That's what _____ said.

3. Steve, _____ you decided what courses you're taking?

4. He picked _____ children up.

5. I wish I could help _____

6. I should _____ registered my car.

7. _____ _____ running in the marathon?

8. _____ _____ car be ready by this evening?

CD 2; Track 42 Now repeat these sentences after the speaker.

Exercise 7

CD 2; Track 43 Link verb endings with reduced pronouns. Practice the dialogs with a partner, with your teacher, or with the speakers on audio.

Example: confused him

        (confuse-dəm)   *not*   confused/him

1.   **A:** Why was everyone upset with John?

blame-dəm   **B:** Everyone blamed him for losing the game.

2.   **A:** What happened to your bags?

check-təm   **B:** Oh . . . I already checked them in.

3.   **A:** Did Gloria find a ride to school?

drop-tər   **B:** Yeah. Her brother dropped her off.

4.   **A:** Did you get your tests back already?

hand-zəm   **B:** Yeah. That teacher's a grading machine. She always hands them right back.

5.   **A:** I haven't seen Lisa in ages.

keep-sər   **B:** I know. I haven't either. I guess her new job keeps her busy.

6.   **A:** How is your sister's new baby?

watch-tər   **B:** Great! I watched her last Saturday while Lisa and her husband went out.

7.   **A:** How do you know Jim?

interview-dəm   **B:** Actually, I interviewed him for a job.

8.   **A:** What did that man just say to Kate?

ask-tər   **B:** I'm not sure, but I think he just asked her for change.

A Helpful Hint

The words *can't* and *can* are easy to confuse. English speakers rely primarily on stress.

Examples: I CAN'T TRUST him. *(2 stressed words)*

I /kən/ TRUST him. *(1 stressed word)*

The word *can't* is stressed. It has a long, clear /æ/ sound: /kænt/

The word *can* is unstressed. It has a reduced vowel: /kən/

Or, it has no vowel sound: /kn/

Exercise 8

CD 2; Track 44

Listen to the first verse of this chant. How many strong beats are in each line?

CAN YOU DO ME A FAVOR?

Verse 1: Can you do me a favor?
    I can do you a favor.

    Can you open the door?
    I can open the door.

    Can you turn out the light?
    I can turn out the light.

    Can you make it all right?
    I can make it all right.

In the second verse below, underline the strong beats. Then practice with your class. Half of the class asks the questions and the other half answers.

Verse 2: Can you take me to work?
    I can take you to work.

    Can you fly me to France?
    I can fly you to France.

    Can you teach me to dance?
    I can teach you to dance.

    Can you make it all right?
    I can make it all right.

With a partner, write a third verse. Follow the format of Verses 1 and 2. Share the new verse with the class.

Verse 3: Can you do me a favor?
I can do you a favor.

Can you _____ ?

_____ .

_____ ?

_____ .

_____ ?

_____ .

A Helpful Hint

Remember that native speakers of English intentionally reduce function words, so you will not hear all words clearly. Don't worry when this happens. Pay attention to the stressed parts of the message and you can usually get the basic meaning.

Exercise 9

CD 2; Track 45

Listen to your teacher or the speaker on audio say the sentences below. Circle *can* or *can't, were* or *weren't*.

1. I (can / can't) call you tomorrow.

2. I (can / can't) watch your children tonight.

3. She (can / can't) meet with me today.

4. He (can / can't) make an appointment tomorrow.

5. He (can / can't) come to the party.

6. I (can / can't) be there on time.

7. Phil (can / can't) drive tonight.

8. The missing books (were / weren't) found.

9. After walking five miles, we (were / weren't) tired.

10. You (were / weren't) told to do that.

Check your answers with your teacher.

With a partner, take turns saying the sentences above with *can* or *can't*. Your partner should respond in a way that shows understanding.

Example: Student A: I (can / can't) go to the game.

Student B: Too bad! Why not?

Student A: Unfortunately, I have to study.

Switch roles and repeat.

Communicative Practice: Scheduling an Appointment

InfoGap

With a partner, practice rhythm patterns as you schedule a business appointment.

Step 1: Preview the rhythm patterns in the sample sentences below. Pay special attention to *can* and *can't*.

I can MEET on MONday at TEN.

I can MEET from TWO to THREE.

I CAN'T MEET then. I'm GOing to the DENtist.

Can you MEET at TWELVE?

I'm BUsy from ONE to TWO.

WHAT about FRIday at TEN?

Step 2: Choose one of the following sets of roles. Decide who will play *role A* and who will play *role B*.

_____ **A.** Software consultant

B. Client (Bank of the North)

_____ **A.** Dean of Students

B. Student government representative

_____ **A.** Graphic designer (Quick Copy Shop)

B. Client (Dave's Landscape Service)

_____ **A.** Accountant

B. Client (Owner of My Thai Restaurant)

Step 3: Write the purpose of the appointment: _____

Step 4: *Role A:* Use the schedule on the next page. *Role B:* Turn to the schedule on page 210. Fill in the *shaded* boxes with appointments typical for your role. Leave the unshaded boxes empty. Choose from the commitments below and create your own.

LIST OF COMMITMENTS		
conference call	workshop	exam
seminar	lunch meeting	car to mechanic
in-service training	dentist	pronunciation class

Step 5: Sit back-to-back, call your partner, tell your partner why you want to meet, and find a time when you are both available.

SCHEDULE/ROLE A

Time	Monday	Tuesday	Wednesday	Thursday	Friday
9:00					out of town
10:00					
11:00		interview			
12:00			staff meeting		
1:00					
2:00				conference	
3:00					
4:00					

Extend Your Skills . . . to Recording a Message

You have just bought a new answering machine for your home or office. Write a message for your new machine. Circle the content words (or the stressed syllables of the content words).

Message:

_____

_____

_____

_____

_____

_____ (BEEP!)

Record your message. Listen to the recording and evaluate your rhythm patterns. Are your stressed words and syllables longer and stronger than your unstressed words and syllables?

Oral Review: Rhythm in Phrases and Sentences

Schedule an individual consultation with your teacher, complete the review as a group project, or submit a recording. Mark the stressed words and syllables in these famous quotations. Read them with special attention to rhythm patterns.

WORDS OF WISDOM

1. A little learning is a dangerous thing. —Alexander Pope

2. Laughter is inner jogging. —Norman Cousins

3. You are never fully dressed until you wear a smile. —Charley Willey

4. Those who cannot remember the past are condemned to repeat it.
   —George Santayana

5. It usually takes me more than three weeks to prepare a good impromptu *expontanous*
   speech. —Mark Twain

6. I can resist everything except temptation. —Oscar Wilde

7. No one has ever become poor by giving. —Anne Frank

8. The only thing we have to fear is fear itself. —Franklin D. Roosevelt

Listen to your recording before you submit it. Did you emphasize the stressed words and syllables? Did you reduce the unstressed syllables and function words?

BEYOND THE PRONUNCIATION CLASSROOM

Knock! Knock! Jokes
Knock! Knock! jokes are often based on reduced words and linking. These jokes are one way young children who are learning English as a *first* language become aware of reduced speech.

Pronunciation Point: Rhythm, reduced words, and linking

Task: Ask a friend who learned English as a child if she or he knows a Knock! Knock! joke. Ask the friend to teach you one or two favorites. Write the jokes down.

Before: In small groups, analyze these jokes. What words are reduced? What words are linked? With a partner, practice telling the jokes.

X: Knock! Knock!	**X:** Knock! Knock!	**X:** Knock! Knock!
Y: Who's there?	**Y:** Who's there?	**Y:** Who's there?
X: Letter.	**X:** Oliver.	**X:** The Sultan.
Y: Letter who?	**Y:** Oliver who?	**Y:** The Sultan who?
X: Letter in. _Let her in._ It's cold out here.	**X:** Oliver _____ friends are coming over.	**X:** The Sultan _____ Pepper.

After: Bring jokes to class. Be prepared to teach a joke.

Thought Groups and Focus Words

Fluent speakers organize their speech into phrases or **thought groups**.

They speak thought by thought.

They. Do. Not. Speak. Word. By. Word.

Thought groups make information easier for the listener to understand. Read these examples. Pause briefly at the end of each thought group.

Phone number: 202 / 555 / 1212
Sentence: Some of my best friends / are people I've met in class.

Every thought group has a **focus word:** one key word with more emphasis than the others.

Some of   my   BEST   **FRIENDS** /are   PEO   ple I've   MET   in   **CLASS**.

You might hear other stressed words in a thought group, but generally you will hear only one focus word.

In this chapter, you will learn about dividing speech into thought groups. You will also learn about highlighting the key word or focus word in each thought group.

Listen!

Listening Activity 1

CD 2; Track 46

Listen to your teacher or the speaker on audio say the phrases. If you hear one thought group, circle ☝. If you hear two thought groups, circle ✌. The first one has been done.

1. a. seven-week-long vacations   ☝

    b. seven / week-long vacations   ✌

2. a. three-hour-long tests

   b. three / hour-long tests

3. a. thirty-nine-cent stamps

   b. thirty / nine-cent stamps

4. a. I don't know George.

   b. I don't know, / George.

5. a. Who's hiring Julia?

   b. Who's hiring, / Julia?

Check your answers with your teacher.

Listening Activity 2

Part A: Close your book and listen to this radio advertisement. Then open your book and listen again for the brief pauses or breaks. Mark the end of each break or thought group with a slanted line (/). The first two have been marked.

CD 2; Track 47

"Unlike other copier companies, / Mita doesn't make cameras, /

or televisions, or calculators, or DVD players, or answering machines,

or vacuum cleaners, or dishwashers, or cell phones, or laptops. The fact

is, Mita doesn't make anything but great copiers. After all, we didn't

become the fastest growing copier company for the last five years by

selling microwave ovens. Mita. All we make are great copiers."

Check your answers with your teacher.

Part B: Listen again. Put a dot • above the focus—the word or syllable with the *most emphasis*—in each thought group. The first two have been done.

CD 2; Track 48

CD 2; Track 49 Unlike other copier companies

CD 2; Track 50 Mita doesn't make cameras

CD 2; Track 51 ... or dishwashers,

CD 2; Track 52 or cell phones,

CD 2; Track 53 or laptops.

CD 2; Track 54 The fact is,

CD 2; Track 55 Mita doesn't make anything

CD 2; Track 56 but great copiers.

Play each track as many times as you wish. Check your answers with your teacher.

Listening Activity 3

CD 2; Track 57 Listen to this dialog between college roommates. Put a dot • above each focus word or the primary stress of each focus word.

Midterm Anxiety

X: I've got to study / and I can't find my book.

Y: Which book?

X: My economics book.

Y: Why don't you try the bookcase?

X: Well, because the bookcase / is full of your photography books.

Y: OK, then check the bedroom.

X: I've already looked in the bedroom. / This apartment's a mess! / I can't find anything in this place.

Y: Hey! / Wait a minute. / The book's right there / — in your hand.

Check your answers with your teacher.

Now listen to the speakers hum the dialog in Listening Activity 3. How do the speakers call attention to the focus of each thought group?

The pitch changes on the stressed syllable of the focus word. The pitch usually jumps up, but sometimes it jumps down.

Rules and Practices 1: Thought Groups

Periods and commas make ideas clear to readers. Thought groups make ideas clear to listeners. How many thought groups are in this sentence?

Woman without her man is helpless.

Some people might say the sentence in two thought groups; others might say it in three.

a. Woman without her man / is helpless. (*2 thought groups*)

b. Woman / without her / man is helpless. (*3 thought groups*)

Who is helpless in each of the sentences?

If you don't break your speech into logical thought groups, you will be hard to understand, no matter how clear each word is.

Rule 8-1

 Thought groups are meaningful groups of words. They usually consist of grammatical units or chunks.

Examples: Short sentences: <u>I've got to study.</u> / <u>Where've I put my book?</u>

Clauses: <u>If you speak in thought groups,</u> / <u>you will be easier to understand.</u>

Phrases: Mita doesn't make anything / <u>except great copiers.</u>

Transitions: <u>The fact is,</u> / thought groups make you sound more fluent.

Expressions: <u>Unfortunately,</u> / I've lost my economics book.

What is the shortest thought group above? What is the longest? What seems to be the average length?

Exercise 1

With a partner, take turns unscrambling the job descriptions. Start with a thought group from Column A. Then add thought groups from Columns B and C. Take turns saying the sentences.

Example: Talk show host Oprah Winfrey / wanted to pursue a speaking career / from the age of 12.

THOUGHT GROUP A	THOUGHT GROUP B	THOUGHT GROUP C
1. Talk show host Oprah Winfrey ✔	started a software company	when she was only 13.
2. Mrs. Field's Cookies founder	wanted to pursue a speaking career ✔	from the age of 12. ✔
3. Microsoft founder Bill Gates	came up with her cookie recipe	when he was only 15.

THOUGHT GROUP A	THOUGHT GROUP B	THOUGHT GROUP C
4. Actress-linguist Lucy Liu	once sold blue jeans	before she became a superstar.
5. Fashion designer Tommy Hilfiger	went to the University of Michigan	from the trunk of his car.
6. Actress-singer Jennifer Lopez	worked in a law office	to study Asian languages.

Exercise 2

Each thought group in parentheses is misplaced. With a partner, show the correct place with this symbol: ∧. Then practice saying the corrected sentences.

Example: A calf was born to a farmer (with two heads).

> *Mark:* A calf ∧ was born to a farmer (with two heads).

> *Say:* A calf / with two heads / was born to a farmer.

1. Please take time to look over the brochure that is enclosed (with your family).

2. The hostess served the dinner to her guests (that she had been warming in the oven).

3. The Toyota hit a utility pole (going about 45 miles per hour).

4. The patient was referred to a psychiatrist (with a severe emotional problem).

5. She died in the home in which she was born (at the age of 88).

6. Here are some suggestions for handling annoying telephone calls (from the New England Telephone Company).

CD 2; Track 60 Say the corrected sentences *with* the teacher or the speaker on audio.

How would *you* divide the lecture segment below? Mark the end of each thought group with /. The first two have been done.

"Let's continue our discussion of pollution / Yesterday / we defined pollution Today we'll talk about the impact of pollution its far-reaching effects Many people think pollution is just a problem for scientists but it's not just a problem for scientists It affects everyone Because it affects human lives it's a health problem Because it affects property it's an economic problem And because it affects our appreciation of nature it's an aesthetic problem"

Now listen to the teacher or the speaker on audio deliver the lecture. Did this speaker pause in the same places?

CD 2; Track 61

Something to Think About

Thought groups can vary from speaker to speaker. Although there is not one correct place to pause, it is important to break up long sentences and to group words that belong together. It is also important to vary the length of your thought groups. Too many short thought groups can make your speech sound choppy.

Rules and Practices 2: Normal or Basic Focus Words

The focus word is the most important piece of information in each thought group. The focus word (or the stressed syllable of the focus word) has a long, clear vowel. Most important, it has a major pitch change, usually a pitch rise.

Example: I was SO **TIRED** / that I SLEPT until **NOON**.

Rule 8-2

☑ *The focus word is normally the last content word of a thought group.*

Example: X: José looks reLIEVED.

Y: That's because he found his WALlet.

CD 2; Track 62

Function words following focus word are backgrounded.

Example: X: What do you think about the fare increase?

Y: I don't know. I haven't HEARD about it.

Exercise 4

With a partner, put a dot • over the last content word in each thought group. The first two have been done.

1. **A:** Why did Carlos take a cab? **B:** Because he missed the last train.
2. **A:** Excuse me. Where is the manager? **B:** Just a minute. I'll get her.
3. **A:** Look! Bae's here. **B:** Yeah. I'm going to lunch with him.
4. **A:** What do you hear from Jing? **B:** I haven't been able to reach her.
5. **A:** Let's meet in front of the restaurant. **B:** OK. I'll be waiting for you.
6. **A:** Is something wrong with your salad? **B:** Well, it looks like there's a bug in it.
7. **A:** I'm going to need Peter's e-mail. **B:** OK. I'll ask him for it.
8. **A:** Where was Miriam's book? **B:** It was in her hand!
9. **A:** How was the exam? **B:** Well, I did better than I thought I would.
10. **A:** I don't have enough cash. **B:** I guess we'll have to get some.

Check your answers. Practice with a partner.

CD 2; Track 63 Repeat the sentences after your teacher or the speakers on audio. Nod your head slightly as you say each focus word.

Rule 8-3

✔ ***When the focus is a compound or multi-syllable word, the pitch change is on the primary stress of the focus word.***

CD 2; Track 64

Examples: (autoMATic) Don't worry. This transmission is autoMATic.

(diRECtion) Things are moving in the right diRECtion.

(MAILbox) I haven't checked my MAILbox yet.

(CREdit card) How did you lose your CREdit card?

Exercise 5

With a partner, identify the last content word in each thought group. Put a dot •
over the syllable with primary stress. The first two have been done. Take turns
practicing the sentences.

1. I completely agree with your priorities.

2. We're excited about collaborating on this.

3. That's a tremendous amount of responsibility.

4. The teacher wants us to record it.

5. They're predicting a huge snowstorm.

6. I can't seem to access my address book.

7. Come to think of it, / Kate's a vegetarian.

8. Jessie's at the post office / getting a money order.

Check your answers. Practice with a partner.

CD 2; Track 65
Repeat the sentences after your teacher or the speaker on audio. Again, nod your
head slightly as you say each focus word.

Rules and Practices 3: Special or Marked Focus Words

Sometimes focus shifts to a word other than the last content word, depending
on the context or the intent of the speaker. This is special focus.

Examples: X: José needs to find his wallet. Y: He FOUND his wallet.

X: Did José find your wallet? Y: No. He found HIS wallet.

Rule 8-4

✔ *Focus highlights words that contrast with each other.*

CD 2; Track 66
Example: I have some BAD news/ and some GOOD news.

"Not only do I want a cracker—we all want a cracker!"

In order to signal a contrast, sometimes we emphasize function words that are not normally stressed.

Example: X: Are you and your girlfriend going to the wedding?

                  ●   ●

        Y: SHE'S going, but I'M not.

In order to signal a contrast, sometimes we emphasize syllables that are not normally stressed.

Example: X: Will the report be finished by Friday?

                                ●   ●

        Y: Ahmed thinks it's POSsible, / but I think it's IMpossible.

Speakers might signal a contrast with an extra high pitch.

Example: I went to Rome, GEORgia, but Rita went to Rome, ITaly.

Exercise 6

With a partner, put a dot • above the focus word (or stressed syllable of the focus word) in these contrasts. The first one has been done.

1. I'm looking for a used car, / not a new one.
2. This isn't the twenty-fifth floor; / it's the twenty-sixth floor.
3. He found his debit card / but not his credit card.
4. I made the check out to John Nelson / instead of Joan Nelson.

5. I thought our anniversary was on the fourteenth, / but it's on the fifteenth.

6. He doesn't need the white pages; / he needs the yellow pages.

7. That's my home number. / Let me give you my cell number.

8. This is my sister, Silvia Gomez, / and my brother, Louis Gomez.

9. If the clothes aren't on the dryer, / look in the dryer.

10. I was more interested in hearing his opinion / than in giving mine.

Check your answers.

Repeat after your teacher or the speakers on audio.

CD 2; Track 67

Add movement to your practice: Roll up an 8 ½" x 11" piece of paper. Lightly tap the paper on the desk as you say the focus word or syllable. Or high-five your partner.

Example: I'm looking for a USED car, / not a NEW one.

Rule 8-5

☑ *Focus highlights new information.*

Example: X: What's your favorite desSERT?

CD 3; Track 1

Y: Probably ICE cream.

X: But what KIND of ice cream?

Y: Oh, definitely CHOColate ice cream.

Notice that old or repeated information is backgrounded.

Exercise 7

In pairs, put dots • over focus words (or the primary stress of the focus words) in the dialogs.

Example: X: I hear you have a new aPARTment.

       Y: Yeah. It's in the East BAY.

       X: Oh. WHERE in the East Bay?

       Y: In AlaMEda. It's a little less exPENsive there.

       X: How's your comMUTE? Is it BETter?

       Y: Oh, MUCH better.

1. *Dialog: DEADLINES*

    X: What's the matter?

    Y: Well, I'm stuck on this assignment.

    X: What kind of an assignment?

    Y: Oh, it's a paper. A philosophy paper. And it's due tomorrow.*

2. *Dialog: LOST AND FOUND*

    X: Look at these sunglasses. Aren't they great?

    Y: Hmm. Where did you get those sunglasses?

    X: I found them.

    Y: Well, I hate to tell you this, / but I think they're my sunglasses.

3. *Dialog: THE PARTY*

    X: I'm getting confused about dates. When's the party?

    Y: Which party?

    X: You know . . . the staff party.

    Y: Oh. It's the twenty-fifth. Tuesday night.

    X: But there's supposed to be a meeting on Tuesday night.

    Y: Actually, that's been postponed.

*Final time adverbials like *today* and *tomorrow* are not usually prominent unless time is the focus.

    What're you going to do today?   *(the activity is the focus of the statement)*

    My paper's due today!   *(time is the focus of the statement)*

4. *Monolog: OPENING A PRESENT*

    X: Hmm . . . this feels like a book.

       Oh good! It's a cookbook.

       An Italian cookbook!

5. *Monolog: WHAT'S FOR DINNER?*

    X: Uh-oh. It smells like spinach.

       I hate spinach.

       Oh . . . it's broccoli. Good. I love broccoli.

To check your answers, listen to the teacher or the speakers on audio say the dialogs. Practice the dialogs with a partner. Then choose one dialog above. Modify it in any way you would like. Mark the focus words. Practice the dialog until you can say it without reading it.

CD 3; Track 2

Exercise 8

With a partner, put a dot • above the focus word or primary stress of the focus word in each thought group. The first three have been done.

>   •   •   •
>
> "Let's continue our discussion of pollution. / Yesterday / we defined pollution. /
>
> Today / we'll talk about the impact of pollution / its far-reaching effects. / Many people
>
> think pollution is just a problem for scientists / but it's not just a problem for scientists. /
>
> It affects everyone. / Because it affects human lives, / it's a health problem. / Because
>
> it affects property, / it's an economic problem. / And because it affects our appreciation
>
> of nature, / it's an aesthetic problem."

Check your answers.

Now say the lecture chorally with the teacher or the speaker on the audio. Replay the track several times.

CD 3; Track 3

Rule 8-6

 Focus corrects or modifies a previous statement.

Example: X: Lunch is at twelve-thirty.

Y: Actually, I heard it was at one-thirty.

CD 3; Track 4

Something to Think About

The word *actually* serves an important function in conversation. If you introduce a correction with *actually*, you will sound more polite and less abrupt:

Example without "actually":

A: HI, Karen.

B: It's KAra.

Example with "actually":

A. HI, Karen.

B. ACtually, it's KAra.

Exercise 9

Student A: Say the incorrect statements below.

Student B: Correct the statements. If you are *certain* of your correction, introduce it with *actually*. If you are *not quite certain,* choose another expression from the box.

ACtually, . . .	I'm **PRET**ty sure . . .	I'm almost **CER**tain . . .
I was under the impression . . .	I don't **THINK** so . . .	**I** always thought . . .

Example: A: Classes begin on the eighth of SepTEMber.

B: I'm almost CERtain they begin on the NINTH (of September).

1. Dante wrote Hamlet.
2. Smoking decreases your risk of heart disease.
3. The Taj Mahal is in Thailand.
4. Ecology is the study of personality.
5. The Amazon River is the longest river in the world.
6. CO_2 is the chemical symbol for water. *di ox ide*
7. The Atlantic Ocean is to the west of the United States. *east*

8. Kyoto is the capital of Japan.

9. Monet was a famous Dutch painter.

10. George Washington was the second president of the United States.

 Switch roles and do the exercise again. This time monitor your partner's use of focus.

CD 3; Track 5   Listen to the suggested corrections on audio.

Rule 8-7

Sizes

☑ *Focus emphasizes agreement.*

CD 3; Track 6

Example: X: This chapter's easy.

            Y: It is easy.

When signaling agreement, we usually emphasize the verb "to be" or the auxiliary.

Example: X: He's such a great cook. He should think about opening a restaurant.

            Y: You're right. He should (think about that).

Exercise 10

In groups of three, use focus to agree or disagree. *Student 1* expresses an opinion. *Students 2* and *3* close their books and respond by agreeing or disagreeing. Responses should be truthful.

Example: Student 1:   I think that . . . the Honda's the best car on the road.

           Student 2:   I agree. It is (the best car).

           Student 3:   I think the Smart Car's the best.

Student 1: I think that . . .

1. Paris is the most beautiful city in the world.

2. Everyone should have three-day weekends.

3. Writing English is easier than speaking it.

4. All guns should be illegal.

5. *Star Wars* is the best movie ever made.

6. Your opinion on a topic: _____

Note: See Appendix D for a summary of the Guidelines for Focus.

Prime-Time Practice

Focus Words in Running Speech

CD 3; Track 7 — An international graduate student in business talks about her program. Listen and repeat each phrase until you can match the timing, thought groups, and pitch jumps on the focus words.

CD 3; Track 8 — Most of the classes / are evening / and afternoons

CD 3; Track 9 — where a majority of students / come straight from work

CD 3; Track 10 — and my assumption was

CD 3; Track 11 — that . . . uh . . . they'll just come to class

CD 3; Track 12 — get it over with / and then after class

CD 3; Track 13 — just leave / and go home

CD 3; Track 14 — because they've had a busy day

CD 3; Track 15 — and would not be really interested in socializing

CD 3; Track 16 — getting to know anybody / making friends.

CD 3; Track 17 — And I was wrong.

CD 3; Track 18 — Some of my best friends / are people I've met in class.

Record yourself reading the passage. Monitor thought groups and focus. Make corrections at the end of the recording.

Follow-up to Prime-Time Practice: Use the Internet to practice focus in authentic spoken English. Web sites that have audio and transcripts are especially useful. An example is *Movie Trailers with Scripts:* www.english-trailers.com/index.php.

Listen to the trailer without the script, paying special attention to focus. Listen several times more to mark • the focus words on the script. Then use the script to speak with the speaker. Match your words, timing, and intonation to the speaker's.

Exercise 11

CD 3; Track 19

Say each question and response with the speakers on audio, or practice with a partner, as follows:

Student A: Ask question **a.** or **b.** Monitor your partner's response.

Student B: Cover the questions and respond using the correct focus word or syllable.

QUESTIONS (STUDENT A)	RESPONSES (STUDENT B)

Examples:

a. What did you do last night?   I called my mother.

b. You should call your mother.   I called my mother.

a. You look relaxed.   I just got back from a long vacation.

b. You need a long vacation.   I just got back from a long vacation.

1. a. How about some dinner?   Let's get a medium cheese pizza.

b. How about a medium mushroom pizza?   Let's get a medium cheese pizza.

2. a. What happened?   I sprained my ankle.

b. Did you break your ankle?   I sprained my ankle.

3. a. Did you mail that memo?   No, I faxed it.

b. Did John fax that memo?   No, I faxed it.

4. a. Did you say 929?   I said 925.

b. Did you say 525?   I said 925.

5. a. Where are you from?   Near Rio.

b. Are you from Rio?   Near Rio.

Exercise 12

TOEFL® iBT Speaking Practice *(Optional)*

One of the independent speaking tasks on the TOEFL® iBT might require that you express a preference. This task often involves highlighting contrasts.

Examples: PERsonally, I'd rather live in a TEMperate climate / than a TROpical climate.

For most things, I'd rather buy from a STORE than onLINE.

1. Before you begin:

- Have available recording equipment and a timepiece with a second hand.
- Take about 15 seconds to prepare a response to the question in the box. You may use the outline below to help organize your thoughts.
- Then take about 45 seconds to respond.

> "Some students prefer a formal classroom where the teacher lectures and students take notes. Other students prefer an informal classroom where students participate and work in groups. Which type of classroom do you prefer and why? Include details and examples in your response."

Your choice or opinion:

_____

One advantage of the *other* choice:

_____

Two or three reasons for *your* choice:

1. _____

2. _____

3. _____

2. *Examples of Focus Words for Contrasts:*

Some students think it's better to learn from a pro**FES**sor / than from other **STU**dents /...that it's more ef**FI**cient. /Well, that might be true for **THEM**, / but it is not true for **ME**. / **MOST** of the time, / I prefer an **IN**formal classroom / to a **FOR**mal classroom.

Communicative Practice:
Announcing Schedule Changes

Student A: You have volunteered to help with international student orientation at your school. Announce the schedule changes on page 211. Rehearse what you will say, and then state the changes to Student B. Signal the changes with the pitch of your voice.

Student B: Mark the changes on the schedule below. Do not look at each other's schedules.

WELCOME TO INTERNATIONAL STUDENT ORIENTATION

August 19

Dean's Welcome   Candler Chapel
9:00–9:30

Immigration Sessions   Student Center, Room 413, F-1 Visa Holders
9:30–10:30   Student Center, Room 355, J-1 Visa Holders

Refreshment Break, 10:30–10:45, Commons

Health Care in the U.S.   Student Center Cinema
10:45–11:45   Student health insurance and
                                       the health care system

Luncheon, 12:00–1:00, Student Center Ballroom

Campus Tours   Tour leaders leave from the lobby of the
1:00–2:30   Student Center.
                                       The last tour departs at 2:00.

Transportation   Student Center Ballroom
3:00–4:00   City and campus transportation systems
                                       and costs

Student B: Check your answers. Tell *Student A* what changes you made.

Oral Review: Thought Groups and Focus Words

Schedule a consultation with your teacher, review in pairs, or submit a recording.

Directions: Mark the focus in each thought group. Record yourself reading the quotes.

LYRICS AND QUOTES

1. I'd rather be a hammer / than a nail.
   —Paul Simon

2. Whoever gossips to you / will gossip about you.
   —Unknown Source

3. We will meet your physical force / with soul force.
   —Martin Luther King, Jr.

4. You cannot escape the responsibility of tomorrow / by evading it today.
   —Abraham Lincoln

5. The earth does not belong to man. / Man belongs to the earth.
   —Chief Seattle

6. We see things not as they are; / we see them as we are.
   —Anaïs Nin

7. That's one small step for a man, / one giant leap for mankind.
   —Neil Armstrong, stepping onto the surface of the moon

8. Genius is 1 percent inspiration / and 99 percent perspiration.
   —Thomas Edison

9. A pessimist thinks the glass is half-empty; / an optimist thinks the glass is half-full.   —Unknown Source

10. Ask not what your country can do for you; / ask what you can do for your country.   —John F. Kennedy

Listen to your recording before you submit it. Did you highlight the focus words. Make corrections at the end of the recording.

BEYOND THE PRONUNCIATION CLASSROOM

Comparing Business Practices

Pronunciation Point: Focus to highlight contrasts

Task: With one or more proficient English speakers, compare business practices in the United States or Canada with those in your country.

Before: Fill in the chart with information about work/business customs of your country. Predict similarities and/or differences that might exist between business customs in your country and those in the United States or Canada.

Area	My Country: _____	United States/Canada
Business Cards		
Handshakes		
Gift Giving		
Dress Codes		
Length of Workday		
Length of Workweek		
Vacation Time		

After: Report on your experience to the class. What were the most interesting similarities or differences? Use focus to highlight contrasts.

Intonation: Falling and Rising Tones

Intonation is the fall and rise of the pitch of the voice. In Chapter 8, you learned how intonation signals the focus word in each thought group or short sentence. You learned that the pitch usually jumps up on the focus word.

> Keiko doesn't like her JOB.

In this chapter, you will learn what happens *after* the pitch jumps on the focus word. Does it fall or rise? It depends on the meaning the speaker wants to communicate.

Keiko doesn't like her JOB.	**fall** = certainty
Keiko doesn't like her JOB?	**rise** = surprise or uncertainty
Keiko doesn't like her JOB / interfering with her STUdies.	**partial fall** = more to come

You will learn other ways rising and falling intonation communicates meaning.

Who does Keiko WORK for?	**fall** = request for information
WHO does she work for?	**rise** = request for clarification

Listen!

Listening Activity 1

CD 3; Track 20 Listen to the teacher or the speakers say the dialog. At the end of each sentence, do you hear falling or rising intonation? Circle ⌄ or ⌄.

DIALOG: ROOM SERVICE

	Falling	Rising
X: May I **HELP** you?		
Y: Yes, I'd like **COF**fee?		
X: You want **CAF?**		
Y: No, I'll have **DE**caf.	⌄	

X: For how **MA**ny?

Y: For **TWO**.

X: What **TIME**?

Y: About **SE**ven.

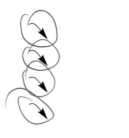 

Check your answers with your teacher. Replay the track if necessary.

Listening Activity 2

CD 3; Track 21

After the pitch jumps on each focus word, does the voice then rise or fall? Listen to the teacher or the speakers on audio. Draw ⬎ or ⬈ after each dot.

Example: We can take a CAB / or a BUS.

1. Would you rather live in a DORM / or a HOUSE?

2. How much should we TIP?

3. Could I get my GRADE?

4. X: What would you like on your SUB?

   Y: I'll have HAM, / BEEF, / and CHEESE.

5. X: The area code is 902.

   Y: Did you say 502?

Compare your answers with those of the other members of the class.

Listening Activity 3

CD 3; Track 22

Your teacher or the speakers on audio will say the statements and responses below.

Circle response **a.** if it sounds like the speaker is *finished*.
            Example: I can't see.
Circle response **b.** if it sounds like the speaker is *continuing*.
            Example: I can't see . . . (paying that much for rent.).

1. What did your teacher do after class?

   a. He passed out.

   b. He passed out . . . (our exam grades).

2. Did you register for biology?

   a. No, I registered for chemistry.

   b. No, I registered for chemistry . . . (because biology was full).

3. What did Dr. Green say?

    a. He said / he doesn't like his students.

    b. He said / he doesn't like his students . . . (coming to class late).

4. Then what did you do?

    a. I turned on the lights.

    b. I turned on the lights . . . (and then I ran downstairs).

5. Could you give me your card number please?

    a. 4307 / 3198 / 4010

    b. 4307 / 3198 / 4010 . . . (8238)

Check your answers. Listen again if desired.

Rules and Practices 1: Intonation at the End of Sentences

Some intonation patterns express attitudes and emotions like anger, doubt, and sarcasm. These patterns are variable and difficult to learn. Others patterns are essential for giving information and participating in discussions and conversations. Several of these patterns are presented below.

Rule 9-1

☑ *Falling intonation at the end of a statement indicates the completion of an idea or sentence. It also expresses certainty.*

CD 3; Track 23

Example: I was accepted at York Uni**VER**sity.

    I start in **JUNE**.

The pitch jumps up on the primary stress of the focus word. If the focus is the last syllable in the sentence, the intonation also glides down on the focus.

    Example: in **JUNE**

If the focus is not the last syllable, the intonation steps down after the focus.

    Example: York Uni**VER**sity

Rule 9-2

✔ *Rising intonation at the end of a statement can indicate surprise, uncertainty, or a desire for confirmation. Speakers expect responses like "yes," "no," or "uh-huh."*

CD 3; Track 24

Example 1: Y: I have some good **NEWS**.

X: You were accepted at **YORK**? *(I think I know, but I want confirmation.)*

Y: Uh-huh. I start in **JUNE**.

Example 2: X: Helen's daughter had a **BA**by last week.

Y: Helen's a **GRANDmother**? *(I'm surprised. She looks so young.)*

X: Yeah. This is her third **GRANDchild**.

The pitch changes on the primary stress of the focus word. Then the intonation rises up from the focus.

Exercise 1

CD 3; Track 25

Practice basic falling and rising intonation. Repeat after your teacher or the speaker on audio.

Part A: *Falling Intonation (completion and certainty)*

1. I lost my **PHONE**.
2. They turned off the **AIR** conditioner.
3. He doesn't know the policy on **SMO**king.
4. John hasn't de**CID**ed yet.
5. The parking lot is **FULL**.
6. He's not feeling any **BET**ter.
7. I need to apply for a new **DE**bit card.
8. I'd like to make an ap**POINT**ment with you.
9. Dr. Westbrook speaks four **LAN**guages.
10. There was another accident on the **IN**terstate.

Note about rising intonation: The pitch change on the focus word may be a jump up (e.g., Helen's a GRANDmother?) or a jump down (e.g. Helen's a GRANDmother?). In either case, the intonation rises up from the focus.

Part B: *Rising Intonation (surprise or uncertainty)*

1. You lost your **PHONE**?

2. They turned off the **AIR** conditioner?

3. He doesn't know the policy on **SMO**king?

4. John hasn't de**CID**ed yet?

5. The parking lot's **FULL**?

6. He's not feeling any **BET**ter?

7. I need to apply for a new **DE**bit card?

8. I need to make an ap**POINT**ment with you?

9. Dr. Westbrook speaks four **LAN**guages?

10. There was another accident on the **IN**terstate?

Practice Part B with a partner. *Student A:* Say the sentence. *Student B:* Respond. Then switch roles.

Example: *Student A:* You lost your **PHONE**?

Student B: Yeah. And it's brand new!

Rule 9-3

 Rising intonation at the end of a statement can also be used to request clarification.

If you want clarification of the entire statement, the pitch rises on or after the last content word.

Example: X: Sergio lost his **JOB**.

Y: He lost his **JOB**?

If you want clarification of a specific item, the pitch rises on or after the item you want clarified.

Example: X: The number is 555–943**5**.

Y: 555-9**4**35? *(Clarify the fourth number.)*

X: Right. **9**435.

Exercise 2

Say these dialogs with the speakers on audio or practice with a partner as follows.

Example: Student A: We'll all meet behind Candler **HALL**.

Student B: Behind **CHAN**dler Hall? *(request for clarification)*

Student A: No, **CAND**ler Hall.

1. A: My e-mail is jdoe@univ.edu.

B: jtoe?

A: No. "D⌣/ as in "dog."

2. A: I'll meet you at 5:45.

B: At 9:45?

A: No. 5:45.

3. A: The cheapest fare is one-thousand, nine hundred dollars.
   B: One-thousand, five hundred?
   A: No, one thousand, nine hundred.

4. A: I'll have a salad with low-fat ranch dressing.
   B: Did you say no-fat ranch?
   A: No, low-fat ranch.

Switch roles and repeat the exercise.

Rule 9-4

☑ *Rising intonation is usually used at the end of yes/no questions.*

If it is a true question and you do not know the answer, use rising intonation.

Example: Hello. Is **JIM** available? *(I don't know the answer.)*

If you use falling intonation for true questions in North American English, you might sound overly serious, authoritative, or intimidating.

Example: Hello. Is Professor **MILLS** available?

☑ *Falling intonation is sometimes used at the end of yes/no questions.*

If you assume you know the answer, you can use falling intonation.

Example: Can you give me an **exAM**ple? *(I assume I know the answer.)*

Falling intonation can also be used when a speaker repeats a yes/no question.

Example : X: Hello. Is **JIM** available?

Y: I'm sorry. Could you re**PEAT** that?

X: Is **JIM** available?

Exercise 3

Part A: Rising Intonation (*I do not know the answer.*)

CD 3; Track 30 Repeat after the teacher or the speakers on audio.

1. Do the buses run after ten o'**CLOCK**?

2. Does Sergio have any va**CA**tion time?

3. Are we going to re**VIEW** today?

4. Did you finish the **TEST**?

5. Is it supposed to **RAIN**?

6. Can you get to Denver by **TRAIN**?

7. Hello. Is **MARK** available?

8. Are you open on **MON**days?

9. Is it po**LITE** / to eat fried chicken with your **FING**ers?

10. Could you **HOLD** for just a minute?

Practice with a partner. *Student A:* Ask the question. *Student B:* Give a response. Then switch roles.

"Can you hang on a sec? I think I just took another picture of my ear."

Part B: Falling Intonation (*I assume I know the answer.*)

CD 3; Track 31 Repeat after the teacher or the speakers on audio.

1. **A:** Let's take the **BUS**.

   B: Yes, but does it run after **MID**night?

2. **A:** Maybe Bae can go to the **BEACH** with us.

   B: Fine, but does he have enough va**CA**tion time?

3. **A:** Hello? Williams **REAL**ty.

   B: Hello. Is **MARK** available?

4. **A:** It would make sense to get a **HY**brid.

   B: True. But can we really af**FORD** one?

5. **A:** Let's take a **WALK**.

   B: I'd like to. But do we have the **TIME**?

6. **A:** I brought all of my **PA**pers.

   B: Did you bring your in**SUR**ance card?

Now practice with a partner. Switch roles and practice again.

Rule 9-5

CD 3; Track 32 Listen to these *wh-* questions. Does the intonation fall or rise at the end?

Examples: Who's at the door?
What does he want?

✔ *The intonation usually falls at the end of wh– questions.*

Example: X: I'm going to the Middle East.

Y: Oh. Where are you **GO**ing? *(request for information)*

X: To Dubai.

✔ *If the speaker is requesting repetition, the intonation rises.*

The intonation rises on the *wh-* word.

Example: X: I'm going to the Middle East.

Y: **WHERE** (are you going)? *(request for repetition)*

X: The Middle East.

Note: In requests, rising intonation is generally considered to be more polite: Would you mind dimming those **LIGHTS?** Could you please re**PEAT** that?

Exercise 4

Student A: Make a statement.
Student B: Respond with a *wh-* word with either a rising or falling intonation.
Student A: Choose the correct response.

Example: *Student A:* I'm going to Brazil.

   Student B: Where?   (or)   Where?

   Student A: Brazil.   (or)   Rio.

1. A: They moved their headquarters near campus.

   B: Where?   (or)   Where?

   A: Near campus.   (or)   On 10th Street.

2. A: I left my umbrella on the bus.

   B: Where?   (or)   Where?

   A: On the bus.   (or)   On the front seat.

3. A: The next game is this weekend.

   B: When?   (or)   When?

   A: This weekend.   (or)   On Saturday afternoon.

4. A: I'll call you in the morning.

   B: When?   (or)   When?

   A: In the morning. (or)   About 9:00.

5. A: There was a terrible earthquake in Turkey.

   B: Where?   (or)   Where?

   A: Turkey.   (or)   Istanbul.

Switch roles and repeat.

Rule 9-6

✔ *We often use rising intonation to check the listener's background knowledge.*

Example: A: You know the **McDONald's** / on **SEcond Street?** (*checking background knowledge*)

CD 3; Track 33

   B: Um-**HMM**.

   A: Well, my apartment's directly across the **STREET.** (*new information*)

Note: The pattern in Rule 9-6 is different from "upspeak," completing *all* thought groups with rising intonation. Upspeak makes speakers sound uncertain. This pattern, however, is used by competent speakers for a specific purpose—to determine knowledge shared by the speaker and the listener.

Exercise 5

Part A: Listen to the teacher or the speaker on audio and repeat.

CD 3; Track 34

Example: A: You know **TeREsa** / in **WRITing class?** *(checking background knowledge)*

B: **YEAH.**

A: You know how she's a **MATH whiz?** *(checking background knowledge)*

B: Um-**HMM.**

A: Well, she got a perfect **SCORE** / on the math **SAT.** *(new information)*

Part B: With a partner, decide whether the intonation rises or falls on/after the focus. Then practice the dialog.

A: You know where the front **ENtrance** is?

B: **YES.**

A: And you remember where the cafe**TEria** is?

B: Uh-**HUH.**

A: OK, walk through all the way through the cafe**TEria,** / and the elevators will be on your **RIGHT.**

Rule 9-7

Listen to this question. How do you know a choice is being offered?

CD 3; Track 35 *Example:* Do you want paper or plastic?

☑ *In questions and statements that give choices, the first alternative has rising intonation and the second has falling intonation.*

Examples: Is the exam to**DAY** / or to**MOR**row?

To **BE** / or **NOT** to be?

Exercise 6

Say these sentences with your teacher or the speaker on audio.

CD 3; Track 36
1. Was the light **YELow** / or **RED?**

2. Is the speed limit 65 / or 70 miles per hour?

3. You should walk on the sidewalk / or on the shoulder.

4. Should we take your car / or mine?

5. Signal a turn with your blinker / or your hand.

6. Should I turn left / or right?

7. Would you rather walk / or ride?

Now write three original sentences that present choices. These should be sentences you would be likely to say. In a small group, take turns saying your sentences.

1. _____

2. _____

3. _____

CD 3; Track 37

Prime-Time Practice

Reading Poetry: The well-known poem "Dream Deferred" by Langston Hughes asks the reader to consider alternatives. Read the poem.

Step 1: Listen to the poem. Pay attention to the use of focus and intonation. Replay several times and read *with* the speaker.

Step 2: Record yourself reading the poem. Rewind your tape and monitor for pitch rise and fall.

In the next class, do a round-robin reading of the poem.

Dream Deferred

What happens to a dream

deferred?

Does it dry up

like a raisin in the sun?

Or fester like a sore —

And then run?

Does it stink like rotten meat?

Or crust and sugar over —

like a syrupy sweet?

Maybe it just sags

like a heavy load.

Or does it explode?

Something to Think About

You have learned a lot of intonation patterns. They are not the only ones in English, but they are some of the most common and useful ones. You are not expected to *memorize* these patterns or even remember them all. It is helpful, however, to be aware of these patterns in the English around you. In time, through listening and practice, you will begin to use many of these patterns automatically.

Decide which intonation patterns are *most* useful in your speaking situations:

1. _____

2. _____

Pay *special* attention to these patterns.

Rules and Practices 2: Intonation at the End of Non-Final Thought Groups

Non-final intonation connects thoughts within sentences. It tells your listener that you want to continue speaking.

If you hear a deep or full pitch fall at the end of a thought group, it is probably a final thought group. The speaker is probably finished with her or his turn.

Example: I can't SEE⟍   **(full fall = finished)**

If you hear a partial fall or rise, it is probably a non-final thought group. The speaker wishes to continue speaking.

Examples: I can't SEE / paying that much for **RENT.** **(partial fall = unfinished)**

I can't SEE / paying that much for **RENT.** **(partial rise = unfinished)**

Note: You may also hear some speakers use a level tone to indicate they wish to continue speaking.

Exercise 7

CD 3; Track 38

Listen. Do you hear a finished or an unfinished idea? Circle **a.** or **b.** The first one has been done.

1. **a.** The food looks **GOOD**.   *Finished*

   b. The food **LOOKS** good . . .   *Unfinished*

2. **a.** Her sister's really **NICE**.   *Finished*

   b. Her **SIS**ter's really nice . . .   *Unfinished*

3. **a.** I speak some **SPAN**ish.   *Finished*

   b. I speak **SOME** Spanish . . .   *Unfinished*

4. **a.** I studied on **SUN**day.   *Finished*

   b. I studied on **SUN**day . . .   *Unfinished*

5. **a.** You can ask for an ex**TEN**sion.   *Finished*

   b. You can **ASK** for an extension . . .   *Unfinished*

Check your answers.

CD 3; Track 39

Listen and repeat both sentences after your teacher or the speaker on the audio. Or do the exercise as a partner practice.

      Student A: Say **a.** or **b.**

      Student B: Circle *Finished* or *Unfinished.*

Check your answers. With your partner, decide what was left unsaid in the unfinished sentences in **b.**

Rule 9-8

   In general, the end of a non-final thought group has a partial fall (or partial rise). This pattern indicates "more to come."

CD 3; Track 40

Example: Her biggest con**CERN**   **(partial fall)**

      is that her neighbor's **WATCH**dog **(partial fall)**

      is so un**FRIEND**ly   **(partial fall)**

      that he might hurt her **CHILD**ren.   **(full fall)**

One of the most common mistakes students make is using a full fall instead of a partial fall at the end of a non-final thought group.

Exercise 8

With a partner, decide the reason for the intonation at the end of each thought group in **Anecdote 1**.

With a partner, decide the intonation at the end of each thought group. The first two have been marked. Take turns practicing **Anecdote 2**.

Anecdote 1

At the end of a fact-filled **SPEECH**,

a **CAN**didate

looked out at his **AU**dience

and **ASKED**,

"Now, are there any **QUES**tions?"

A voice came from the back of the **ROOM**

and **ASKED**,

"Who **ELSE** is running?"

Practice in chorus with your teacher or the speaker on audio.

CD 3; Track 41

Anecdote 2

Prime Minister Winston **CHUR**chill

was a frequent **DIN**ner guest

at the **WHITE** House.

At **DIN**ner one evening,

a woman seated **NEXT** to Churchill

kept complaining about his **PO**licies.

She **TOLD** him,

"If I were your **WIFE**,

I would give you **POI**son."

He re**PLIED**,

"**MA**dam,

if I were your **HUS**band,

I would **TAKE** it."

Practice in chorus with your teacher or the speaker on audio.

CD 3; Track 42

Exercise 9: Intonation on the TOEFL® iBT Speaking Tasks (Optional)

In the speaking section of the TOEFL, you will be asked to give opinions or information, so use these two main intonation patterns:

Full fall = final thought group; finished idea

Partial fall (or rise) = non-final thought group; unfinished idea

Practice these two intonation patterns in the sample response on the next page. This is a sample response from a TOEFL® iBT integrated speaking task. The response concerns the use of cell phones in the classroom. The first three thought groups have been marked.

According to the announcement,

cell phones have to be turned off

before students come in the classroom.

Students aren't even permitted

to put their phones on… uh…silent.

uh

The student understands

why the professor's upset,

but she thinks his policy

is too…uh…too strict.

I guess her biggest reason is

that you…well, students, might need their cell phones

for family emergencies.

Record yourself reading the passage. Evaluate final and non-final intonation. Compare the intonation in the audio recording to the intonation in your response.

CD 3; Track 43

Rule 9-9

Listen to items in a series. How do you know that more items are on the list? How do you know when the speaker has reached the last item?

CD 3; Track 44

Example: I lost my keys, my wallet, my ticket, and my passport.

 When you list two or more items, there is a partial rise on each item except the last.

Example: While you're at the store, / please get **PENS,** / **PAper clips,** / and **FILE folders.**

Exercise 10

With a partner, take turns saying the sentences. Monitor your partner's intonation.

1. The Environmental Protection Agency protects **AIR,** / **SOIL,** / and **WAter.**

2. If I get a new PC, I'll need a table, a printer, and a new monitor.

3. Grades are based on class participation, two papers, and three quizzes.

4. The job benefits include two weeks' paid vacation, six paid holidays, and health insurance.

5. The apartment has a kitchen, a living room, two bedrooms, and a bathroom.

6. Pass a medical building, an apartment building, and a drug store, then turn right.

Exercise 11

Items in a series can be longer than single words. In small groups, choose one situation below and create a response. Mark the focus and intonation as in the example. Then coach a student in your group to give the response to the class.

Example Situation: You want to take a vacation, but several things need to be done before you leave town: *stop the mail, water the plants, ask the neighbor to feed the cat, take out the garbage, and finish cleaning out the refrigerator.* Tell your roommate what three things you will do.

Example Response:

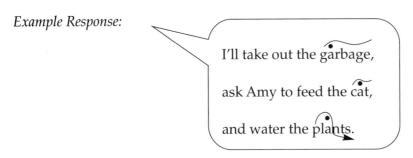

I'll take out the garbage,

ask Amy to feed the cat,

and water the plants.

Situation A. You have been working on a report for two weeks. The deadline is today, but the report is not ready because *the computers have been down, your co-worker Sara has been out of town, and you have had the flu.* In a diplomatic way, ask for an extension and give three good reasons why the extension is justified.

Response:

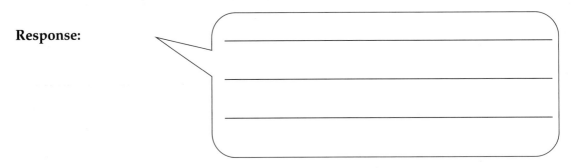

Situation B. It is Saturday afternoon. Your 12-year-old son wants to go to a movie with a friend. However, he neglected his chores for the week (*take out the garbage, straighten his room, cut the grass*). Tell your son what three things he has to do before he can go to the movie.

Response:

Situation C. A travel agent is planning a vacation for you. Here are some typical vacation activities: *hiking, boating, camping, seeing historic sights, visiting museums, and going to the theater.* Tell him three other activities that you enjoy on vacations.

Response: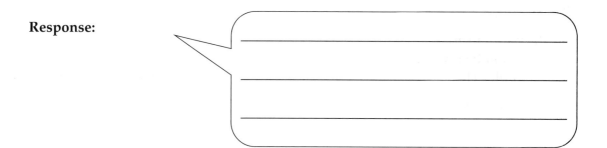

Communicative Practice: Interviews and Surveys

Interview your classmates about the most important technological innovations of the 20th century.

Step 1: Review word stress in the inventions below.

Step 2: Work in pairs. A interviews B. Then reverse roles: B interviews A. Remember intonation for surprise and clarification for follow-up questions (e.g., The computer / has been more beneficial than antibiotics?).

Inventions of the 20th century	Which innovation has affected your daily life the most? How?	Which innovation has been the most beneficial to humankind? How?	Which has been the most harmful? Why?	Total
MIcrowave OVens				
CELL phones				
ComPUters				
AUtomobiles				
TELevision				
ReFRIGerators				
AntibiOTics				
JET planes/ SPACE flight				
INternet				
NUclear WEApons				
GeNETic engiNEERing				

Step 3: In small groups of four or six, report what you learned from your partners. One person in the group should keep a written record. What were the most frequently mentioned innovations?

Oral Review: Final Intonation—Falling and Rising Tones

Name: _____ Date: _____

Schedule an individual consultation with your teacher, complete the review as a group project, or record the review.

Part A: Mark these sentences for intonation patterns. Read the sentences.

    1. A: Eduardo invited 395 people to his wedding!

       B: You're kidding! He invited almost 400 people?

    2. A: I've never been to La Paz Mexican Restaurant. Where is it?

       B: You know the bank / at the intersection of Oak and Main? Well, the restaurant's right behind the bank.

    3. A: Do you like the house?

       B: It's great, / but the biggest drawback / is that my office / is 50 miles away.

Part B: Refer to the technological innovations survey in this chapter. In your opinion, what are the three most important technological innovations of the 20th century? Present the innovations in the form of a list and use the appropriate intonation. Then briefly explain your reason for choosing each one.

Listen to your recording before you submit it. Make corrections at the end of the tape.

BEYOND THE PRONUNCIATION CLASSROOM

Placing a Food Order

Pronunciation Focus: Intonation in questions and items in a series.

Task: Call a restaurant to place a food order for pick-up or delivery.

Before: Bring carry-out menus to class. With a partner, rehearse what you might say, paying special attention to intonation.

    Sample Utterances:

    Do you have any specials?

    Do you deliver or do I have to pick it up?

    What's the total?

    Sorry, I missed that. What's the total?

    You know the school at the corner of Main and First? Turn right there.

After: Discuss your experience with your classmates. Re-create as much of the actual dialogue as you can. Analyze the intonation patterns.

Linking and Connected Speech

In written English, there is space between words.

Do you know what I mean?

In spoken English, there is no space between words.

Yanowhadimean?

Words in a thought group often sound like one long word. It is often difficult to hear where one word ends and the next word begins.

6-7

© 2005 Bil Keane, Inc.
Dist. by King Features Synd.
www.familycircus.com

**"Daddy talks on that when he's
alone. It's his self phone."**

Linking or connecting the end of one word with the beginning of the next word helps gives English its flow. Notice the links between words in this short sentence:

This‿is‿easy.

Remember that linking also helps break up difficult consonant sequences, like *rks* at the end of *works*.

I hope everything wo**rks**‿out.   *sounds like*   work-sout

In this chapter, you will practice making smooth connections between words in thought groups. You will also learn about how sounds change when they are linked.

Listen!

Listening Activity

Listen to the teacher or the speaker on audio say both phrases in each pair using conversational speech. Do you hear a difference?

1.	art class	arc class
2.	phone message	foam message
3.	bad credit	bag credit
4.	made your bed	major bed
5.	eight brothers	ape brothers
6.	six students	sick students
7.	credit or debit	creditor debit
8.	let us	lettuce
9.	beat your team	beacher team
10.	add them	Adam

In conversational speech, the phrases in each pair sound almost the same.

Something to Think About

In Chapter 6, you learned that knock-knock jokes often involve linking and reduced speech. Another type of English humor based on linking and reduced words is book titles and authors. Here are a few examples:

I Love Math by Adam Up	(add them up)
Climbing Mt. Everest by Willie Makit	(will he make it)
Almost Missed the Bus by Justin Time	(just in time)

Rules and Practices: Linking and Sound Change

In conversation, when we link one word with the next, sounds are moved, changed, lost, and added. As a result, spoken English does not always sound the way it is written. The guidelines for linking that follow on the next page will improve your speaking as well as your listening.

Rule 10-1

✔ *When the final consonant sound (C) of one word and the first consonant sound of the next word are the same, the sound is lengthened or held, not pronounced twice.*

CD 3; Track 46

Examples: **C + C (same)**

at_twelve	(hold *t*)
big_game	(hold *g*)
good_deal	(hold *d*)
class_schedule	(lengthen *s*)
he'll_look	(lengthen *l*)

✔ *When the consonant sounds are similar (made in the same place in the mouth), make only one placement for both sounds.*

Examples: **C + C (similar)**

late_dinner

sit_down

come_back

Rule 10-2

✔ *When the final sound is a consonant and the next word begins with a vowel (V) sound, it often sounds like the consonant jumps to the next word.*

CD 3; Track 47

Examples: **C + V**

clean_up	= clea-nup
cleaned_up	= clean-dup
take_off	= ta-koff
drop_him_off	= dro-pi-moff

Exercise 1

Part A: Close your book. Repeat the phrases in the box after your teacher or the speaker on the audio. Then, with a partner, take turns saying each phrase as if it were one word.

CD 3; Track 48

bad_day	some_misunderstanding	graduate_studies	concerned_about_it
good_day	class_schedule	need_time	aware_of_it
speak_clearly	business_school	signed_document	think_it_over
same_message	we'll_leave	white_shirt	turned_it_down

Part B: *Student A:* Check **a.** or **b.** Say that sentence with linking to *Student B.*

Student B: Check the sentence you hear.

1. _____ **a.** She got a car‿on her birthday.

    _____ **b.** She got a card‿on her birthday.

2. _____ **a.** We‿look for the mail delivery.

    _____ **b.** We'll‿look for the mail delivery.

3. _____ **a.** I just base‿it on hearsay.

    _____ **b.** I just based‿it on hearsay.

4. _____ **a.** The police will fine‿him.

    _____ **b.** The police will find‿him.

5. _____ **a.** Did you say‿anything?

    _____ **b.** Did you save‿anything?

6. _____ **a.** Claudio and his brother were‿at Google.

    _____ **b.** Claudio and his brother work‿at Google.

7. _____ **a.** In Montreal, we walk‿everywhere.

    _____ **b.** In Montreal, we walked‿everywhere.

Check your answers. Switch roles. This time mark your sentences with an X.

Rule 10-3

☑ *When the final sound is a stop consonant—/p/, /b/, /k/, /g/, /t/, or /d/—and the next word begins with a consonant, do not release the first stop consonant.*

CD 3; Track 49

Examples: **Stop C+C**

stop‿sign   (do not release /p/)

cab‿driver

big‿problem

lap‿top‿computer

Exercise 2

Repeat these phrases after your teacher or the speaker on audio. Or practice with a partner.

CD 3; Track 50

Examples: take‿control   (hold or lengthen /k/)

take‿out   (move /k/ to the next word)

take‿steps   (do not release /k/)

1. Web_based
   Web_address
   Web_site
   Web_design

2. job_offer
   job_interview
   job_security
   job_description

3. help_pay
   help_provide
   help_out
   help_children

4. keep_pace
   keep_busy
   keep_order
   keep_looking

5. look_closely
   look_good
   look_around
   look_better

6. big_game
   big_impact
   big_difference
   big_mistake

7. add_together
   add_eggs
   add_oil
   add_salt

8. got_tired
   got_dressed
   got_thirsty
   got_sick

Exercise 3

What are three of your all-time favorite movies—films that you would watch over and over? Write the titles below. Practice saying each movie title as if it were one word. Share your titles with your small group or class.

Examples: Lost_in_Translation

Office_Space

Sleepless_in_Seattle

1. _____

2. _____

3. _____

A Helpful Hint

In conversation, the final sounds most likely to change when they are linked are /t/, /d/, and /n/. The /t/, /d/, and /n/ sounds usually become more like the sounds that follow them.

CD 3; Track 51

Examples:　He has eight**_b**rothers.　　(*eight* sounds like *ape*)

He got a ba**d_c**redit rating.　　(*bad* sounds like *bag*)

She left a pho**ne_m**essage.　　(*phone* sounds like *foam*)

Do not worry about making these kinds of changes in your speech. It is much more important to recognize them in the speech of others. You will become more familiar with these changes, however, if you practice saying them.

Exercise 4

The highlighted word in each sentence sounds like one of the words in the box above it. Write the word in the blank.

cheek	cheap

1. a. They cheat by copying other peoples' work.　　　　<u>　cheap　</u>

b. Don't go there. They cheat customers.　　　　<u>　cheek　</u>

ache	ape

2. a. She ate quickly.　　　　<u>　　　　　</u>

b. I already ate breakfast.　　　　<u>　　　　　</u>

quip	quick

3. a. They should quit being so critical.　　　　<u>　　　　　</u>

b. They should quit criticizing his work.　　　　<u>　　　　　</u>

sung	some

4. a. I need some sun protection.　　　　<u>　　　　　</u>

b. I need some sun cream.　　　　<u>　　　　　</u>

CD 3; Track 52　Listen to the teacher or speaker on audio say the sentences above. Practice saying the sentences with a partner.

Rule 10-4

CD 3; Track 53

What sound change do you hear when /t/ is linked with /y/?

Examples: Don't_you know?

Haven't_you heard?

Can't_you go?

✔ **When a word ends in /t/ and the next word begins with /y/, the combined sound is /tʃ/ as in <u>ch</u>oose.**

Example:

sent_you = sen_choo *or* sen_chə

This sound combination is common in negative questions with *you.*

Examples: Don't_you... = don_choo *or* don_chə

Can't_you... = can_choo *or* can_chə

Rule 10-5

CD 3; Track 54

What sound change do you hear when /d/ is linked with /y/?

Examples: Did_you know?

Would_you help?

I called_you.

✔ **When a word ends in /d/ and the next word begins with /y/, the combined sound is /dʒ/ as in <u>j</u>uice.**

Example:

made_your bed = major bed

This sound combination is common in affirmative questions with *you* (e.g., did you . . ., would you . . ., could you . . ., should you . . .).

Examples: Did_you = di_joo *or* di_jə

Could_you = cou_joo *or* cou_jə

Exercise 5

CD 3; Track 55

Dictation. The teacher or the speaker on the audio will say each sentence two times. Write each sentence.

1. _____

2. _____

3. _____

4. _____

5. _____

Check your answers with your teacher. Or see the answer key on p. 225.

Communicative Practice: Driving Test

Use linking as you give your partner an oral driving test.

Step 1: With a partner, preview linking in these phrases:

> should‿you exchange . . .　　how should‿you . . .　　if you start‿to skid . . .
>
> should‿you use . . .　　what should‿you do . . .　　head‿lights . . .
>
> should‿you walk‿on . . .　　set‿your headlights . . .　　involved‿in an‿accident . . .

Step 2: *Student A:* Mark questions 1 through 6 for thought groups (/) below. The first one has been done.

Student B: Mark questions 7 through 12 for thought groups (/) on p. 212. The first one has been done.

Step 3: Practice your questions until the thought groups sound natural and the linking is smooth. Ask your partner the questions. Take notes on your partner's answers.

DRIVING TEST QUESTIONS—*STUDENT A*

1. If there are no sidewalks, / on which side‿of the street / should‿you walk?
2. Unless otherwise posted, what's the maximum speed limit in your state?
3. If your car starts to skid on a slippery surface, should you use the brakes?
4. How should you set your car's headlights in foggy weather?
5. If you are involved in an accident with another driver, what information should you exchange?
6. If you have been drinking alcohol, what should you do before you drive?

Step 4: Report your partner's answers to the class.

Note: Driving laws vary from state to state. Consult the driver's manual for your state if you are not sure about an answer.

A Helpful Hint

English speakers often hesitate while thinking of a word or planning what they want to say. These hesitations, if not excessive, are a normal part of speaking.

If you need to pause, make it brief. If you want to hold the floor while you are thinking, use fillers or hesitation devices. You can use fillers **within** thought groups . . .

Example: Can you hand me the *uuuh* stapler.

　　　　. . . or **as** thought groups.

Example: My ID number is / *I'm not sure* / *let's see* / *I think* N2974T.

Extend Your Skills . . . to a Process Presentation

Explain an interesting process from sports, your daily life, or your field of work or study. Choose a process that has at least three distinct steps and that can be explained clearly in about two minutes (e.g., how to eat Japanese noodles, how to make a snowman, how to make a perfect bowl of popcorn, how to fall asleep quickly and easily).

The presentation will provide an opportunity to use all the skills learned in this course; however, the primary purpose of the explanation is to practice the following:

1. THOUGHT GROUPS: Deliver your ideas in thought groups. Use partial pitch falls for non-final thought groups. Use full pitch falls for final thought groups. Pause after transition words like *first, next, after that*, and *finally* to signal each step of the process. Pause after expressions like *for example* and *in other words*.

2. LINKING: Within thought groups, link your words. Try to keep your speech flowing continuously.

3. PAUSING: Use longer pauses to separate major segments of your presentation (e.g., between each step in your process).

Step 1: Outline your presentation. For each step in your process, tell the audience *what* the step is, *why* it is important, and *how* you accomplish it. Rephrase important information or anything that might be difficult to understand. Use transitions like *in other words* or *to say it another way*.

Step 2: Rehearse your presentation several times, using only your outline. Use a simple, clear, direct speaking style. Use visuals (simple outlines, diagrams, pictures, or flow charts) to add interest and clarity.

Step 3: Record your presentation.

Step 4: Listen to the recording and evaluate your presentation on the form that follows. Submit the form to your teacher.

Process Presentation/Self-Evaluation Form

Name: _____ Topic: _____

Scoring Form: Listen to your recording. Assign 1 point for each component below. You may need to listen to your recording several times.

Part A: Delivery   1 point each

    1. Attention to time limit   _____

    2. Well organized   _____

      • Clear introduction   _____

      • Effective transitions   _____

      • Clear conclusion   _____

    3. Repetition/rephrasing   _____

    4. Interesting   _____

    5. Appropriate level of complexity   _____

                (Part A) _____ × 10 = _____

Part B: Pronunciation/Clarity   1 point each

    1. Clear consonants and vowels in key words   _____

    2. Good stress in key words   _____

    3. Effective rhythm and focus   _____

    4. Appropriate thought groups/ pausing   _____

    5. Adequate speed and volume   _____

                (Part B) _____ × 10 = _____

                TOTAL (Part A + B) = _____

Comments:

_____

_____

_____

_____

_____

Page may be photocopied

Oral Review: Putting It All Together

Name: _____ Date: _____

Schedule an individual consultation with your teacher, complete the review as a group project, or record the review. Choose one of the following: 1) review only linking within thought groups, 2) practice one or two features from previous chapters, or 3) put everything together!

KEY (Use the symbols on this key to mark any text)

Word Stress	=	stressed syllables in capitals (psyCHOlogist)
Rhythm	=	stressed words in capitals (can MAKE a HUGE DIFference.)
Focus Word	=	key words in boldfaced capitals (can MAKE a HUGE **DIF**ference.)
Final Intonation	=	rising ⟋ and falling ⟍ arrows
Linking	=	arc connecting letters (WHAT‿you NAME your **CHILD**)

What's in a Name?

EXperts‿**SAY**

that WHAT‿you NAME your **CHILD**

can‿MAKE a HUGE **DIF**ference. ⟍

A psyCHOlogist‿at UC**LA**

has‿STUdied **NAMES**

and their‿efFECT‿on what we **THINK**‿of people. ⟍

He asked‿THOUsands‿of AMERicans

to reACT‿to CERtain‿**NAMES**. ⟍

ReACTions were VEry **SI**milar. ⟍

For_exAMple,

the name ROCK

got_TOP_MARKS for mascuLInity

but_LOW marks for MORals. ↘

The name_PRUdence

ranked HIGH for moRAlity

but LOW for CHEERfulness. ↘

In GENeral,

PEOple with LONG names

like_AleXANder_and_eLIzabeth

ranked HIGH in sucCESS. ↘

PEOple with SHORT names

like_AMy and JIM

were perCEIVED_as POpular_and FRIENDly. ↘

The SAME was TRUE of NICKnames

like_BOB_for_ROBert

or BILL for WILliam. ↘

BASED_on this REsearch,

WHAT would_YOU name YOUR child? ↘

Listen to your recording before you submit it. Did you use thought groups? Did you link words within thought groups? Did the focus word (or the primary stress of your focus word) stand out? Make corrections at the end of the recording.

Further Practice: Practice saying this passage *with* the speaker over and over. This kind of practice will help *all* aspects of your pronunciation.

Add Movement: Walk the thought groups by stepping on the primary stress of the focus word of each thought group.

BEYOND THE PRONUNCIATION CLASSROOM

Checking Air Fares

Are you, a friend, or a family member planning a trip by air in the near future? Do you need to change a reservation?

Pronunciation Point: Thought groups and linking.

Task: Call the airlines. Verify the lowest available fare you found online. Make or change a reservation, if necessary.

Before: How would you communicate the following sample information? With a partner, predict the interaction:

> This_is (full name)
>
> Could_you tell me / the lowest round_trip_fares from .. to ..
>
> Could_you tell me / the cost to change my ticket?
>
>
> I'd be leaving on <u>(date)</u>   in the (morning, afternoon, evening).
>
> I'd be returning on <u>(date)</u>   in the (morning, afternoon, evening).
>
> OK. / I'd like_to wait. (or). OK / I'd_like to make_a reservation.

Pratice delivering this information in logical thought groups:

Name: _____

Reservation Number: _____

Number and Street: _____

City, State, and Zip Code: _____

Telephone Number: (_ _ _ - _ _ _ - _ _ _ _)

Type of Credit Card: _____

Name on Card: _____

Card Number*:   (_ _ _ _ - _ _ _ _ - _ _ _ _ - _ _ _ _)

Expiration Date: (_ _ / _ _)
                        mo/yr

After: Report on your experience to the class.

*When practicing, make up a 16-digit number.

Consonant Supplements

Supplement 1: The Phonetic Alphabet

We use special symbols to represent the 24 consonant sounds of English. A list of the phonetic symbols with their key words is below.

Exercise 1

CD 3; Track 56

Repeat the sounds and key words after your teacher or the speaker on audio.

/p/ **p**ie	/f/ **f**an	/ʃ/ **sh**oe	/ŋ/ ri**ng**
/b/ **b**uy	/v/ **v**an	/ʒ/ u**s**ual	/l/ **l**ed
/t/ **t**ime	/θ/ **th**ink	/tʃ/ **ch**oose	/r/ **r**ed
/d/ **d**ime	/ð/ **th**em	/dʒ/ **j**uice	/w/ **w**e
/k/ **k**ey	/s/ **s**o	/m/ **m**y	/y/ **y**ou
/g/ **g**o	/z/ **z**oo	/n/ **n**o	/h/ **h**ow

a. Most symbols look like alphabet letters. Some do not. Write the ones that do not.

_____ _____ _____ _____ _____

b. Circle the consonant sounds you do not have in your first language.

c. List any consonant sounds that are difficult for you. You can refer to your *Speech Profile Form* in Chapter 1.

_____ _____ _____ _____

Now that you have been introduced to the sounds, you will learn how they are made.

When you have difficulty making a consonant sound, it is usually because you don't know:

1. Whether the sound is **voiceless** or **voiced;**

2. How the sound is made; that is, whether the air stops or is continuous;

3. Where the sound is made; that is, which parts of the speech pathway touch or almost touch.

Supplement 2: Voiceless and Voiced Sounds:
/p/ *pie* – /b/ *buy*, /t/ *time* – /d/ *dime*, /k/ *back* – /g/ *bag*

Consonants sounds are voiceless or voiced. When you say a voiceless sound, the vocal cords do not vibrate. When you say a voiced sound, the vocal cords vibrate.

Something to Think About

Many students confuse voiceless and voiced sounds.

| I had a <u>c</u>lass. | *might sound like* | I had a <u>g</u>lass. |
| Could you ba<u>g</u> it up? | *might sound like* | Could you ba<u>ck</u> it up? |

The primary difference between the consonant pairs in the exercise below is whether they are voiceless or voiced.

Exercise 1

CD 3; Track 57

Repeat the sound/word pairs below. To check for voicing, place your hands on your cheeks. Feel the vibration as you say the voiced sounds.

VOICELESS CONSONANTS	VOICED CONSONANTS
/p/ **p**ath	/b/ **b**ath
/t/ **t**ime	/d/ **d**ime
/k/ **c**ame	/g/ **g**ame
/f/ **f**an	/v/ **v**an
/θ/ **th**in /θɪn/	/ð/ **th**en /ðɛn/
/s/ **S**ue	/z/ **z**oo
/ʃ/ **sh**oe	/ʒ/ u**s**ual
/tʃ/ **ch**eap	/dʒ/ **J**eep

Except for the voiceless /h/, the remaining consonants sounds are voiced: /m/, /n/, /ŋ/, /l/, /r/, /y/, and /w/.

Consonant Rule 1

☑ *At the ends of words, vowels sound longer before voiced consonant sounds.*

Exercise 2

CD 3; Track 58

Listen to your teacher or the speaker on audio say the word pairs below. Circle the word in each pair that seems to have a longer vowel sound.

1.	rip	(rib)		**7.**	proof	prove
2.	code	coat		**8.**	half	have
3.	save	safe		**9.**	wrote	rode
4.	age	H		**10.**	great	grade
5.	face	phase		**11.**	caused	cost
6.	blog	block		**12.**	rich	ridge

Check the answer key.

CD 3; Track 59   Repeat the word pairs above.

Consonant Rule 2

☑ *At the beginning of words and stressed syllables, voiceless consonants are pronounced with aspiration—the sound of escaping air.*

Exercise 3

CD 3; Track 60

Listen to your teacher or the speaker on audio say the pairs of words below. Circle the word in each pair with the consonant that has more aspiration, that is, sound of escaping air.

1.	view	(few)		**6.**	cold	gold
2.	face	vase		**7.**	drip	trip
3.	bush	push		**8.**	town	down
4.	park	bark		**9.**	cheap	Jeep
5.	Greg	Craig		**10.**	chain	Jane

Check the answer key.

A Helpful Hint

When you practice words and stressed syllables that start with /p/, /t/, and /k/, hold a tissue in front of your mouth. The aspiration or puff of air should make the tissue move. You can also hold your hand in front of your mouth. You should feel a strong puff of air on your hand.

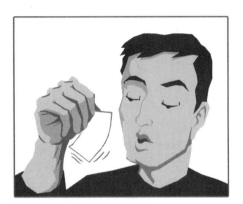

push

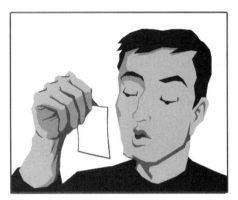

bush

Exercise 4

CD 3; Track 61

Put your hand or a tissue in front of your mouth. Repeat the phrasal pairs below. Pay special attention to the sound and feel of the aspiration in the italicized (voiceless) sounds.

VOICELESS (ASPIRATED)	VOICED (UNASPIRATED)
t	**d**
slow *t*rip	slow drip
stopped the *t*rain	stopped the drain
spare *t*ime	spare dime
p	**b**
*p*ack it up	back it up
California *p*eaches	California beaches
an excellent *p*ie	an excellent buy
k	**g**
tough *c*rime	tough grime
a large *c*lass	a large glass
super *c*lue	super glue

Supplement 3: Continuants and Stops: /s/ *nice* – /t/ *night*

Continuants: Say *f-f-f*. Say *s-s-s*. The air stream is only partially blocked. It moves out of the mouth without stopping. Because the air stream continues without stopping, these consonant sounds are called continuants. Most consonants sounds in English are *continuants*.

Stops: Say /p/. Say /t/. The air stream stops; it is completely blocked. Then it may be released. Because the air stream stops when we say these sounds, these consonant sounds are called *stops*. There are only six English stops: /p/, /b/, /t/, /d/, /k/, /g/.

/s/ in ni<u>c</u>e — The air flow continues.

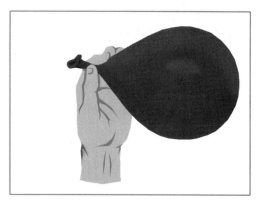

/t/ in nigh<u>t</u> — The air flow stops.

Something to Think About

Students sometimes confuse continuants and stops.

He's a ni<u>c</u>e person.	*might sound like*	He's a nigh<u>t</u> person.
She'<u>s</u> gone.	*might sound like*	She'<u>d</u> gone.

CD 3; Track 62

Listen to the longer duration of the final continuants compared to the shorter duration of the final stops.

CONTINUANTS	STOPS
mi**ss**	mi**tt**
sen**se**	sen**t**
stay**s**	stay**ed**

Exercise 1

Repeat the word and phrase pairs. Then listen to the teacher say one from each pair. Check the one you hear.

CD 3; Track 63

CONTINUANTS (LONGER)	STOPS (SHORTER)
1. _____ bo**ss**	_____ boug**ht**
2. _____ lea**f**	_____ lea**p**
3. _____ presen**ce**	_____ presen**t**
4. _____ dea**th** rates	_____ deb**t** rates
5. _____ last pla**ce**	_____ last pla**te**
6. _____ rai**se** funds	_____ rai**d** funds
7. _____ bo**th** trips	_____ boa**t** trips
8. _____ a noi**se**	_____ annoye**d**

Stop + Continuant: Two consonant sounds in English combine a stop plus a continuant: /dʒ/ as in *joke* and /tʃ/ as in *choke*.

1. /dʒ/ in *joke* — First, stop the air stream with /d/, and then release into /ʒ/.

2. /tʃ/ in *choke* — First, stop the air stream with /t/, and then release it into /ʃ/.

Some students confuse the sounds in *cash* /ʃ/ and *catch* /tʃ/. When you say /ʃ/ in *cash*, the air stream continues. When you say /tʃ/ in *catch*, the air stream stops, and then continues. See *A Helpful Hint* in Chapter 3 on page 23. Or turn to *Consonant Supplement 7* for more practice with these sounds.

Supplement 4: The Speech Pathway and the Consonant Chart

The diagram below shows the speech pathway. The path begins in the lungs where the air stream begins and then continues through the mouth or nose.

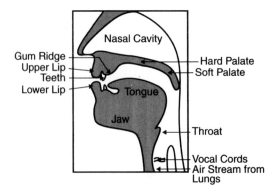

What parts of the speech pathway stop the air stream or let small amounts of air pass through? What parts of the speech pathway touch or almost touch? Look across the top of the chart below and you will see which speech organs are used to produce the consonant sounds. Because speaking is rapid and dynamic, however, positions for sounds will vary depending on the speaker, the surrounding sounds, and the formality of the situation.

CONSONANT CHART

	Both Lips	Lower Lip-Upper Teeth	Tongue-Teeth	Tongue-Gum Ridge	Tongue-Hard Palate	Tongue-Soft Palate	Throat
Stops – Breath is stopped and released.	p/**b**			t/**d**		k/**g**	
Fricatives – Breath is constricted.		f/**v**	θ/**ð**	s/**z**	ʃ/**ʒ**		h
Affricates – Breath is stopped and constricted.					tʃ/**dʒ**		
Nasals – Breath is released through the nose.	**m**			**n**		**ŋ**	
Liquids – Breath is not obstructed.				**l**	**r**		
Glides – Mouth glides from one position to another.	**w**					**y**	

Note: In this chart, the sounds in bold are voiced.

Follow-up: The Web site below shows you how to pronounce the consonant sounds of English. Locate the sound you want to practice. Put a small mirror next to the computer screen so you can see yourself. Imitate speaker's mouth shape and tongue placement. www.uiowa.edu/~acadtech/phonetics/english/frameset.html

Something to Think About

 As you practice some of the more troublesome sounds on the next page, remember that the most important sounds in any utterance are those in the key or focus words.

The following section provides concentrated practice with some of the most problematic consonant sounds for high intermediate/advanced speakers of English. If you want more practice with consonant sounds, *Well Said Intro* provides practice with /p/, /b/; /t/, /d/; /k/, /g/; /m/, /n/, /ŋ/; /θ/; /ʃ/, /tʃ/, /dʒ/; /l/, /r/; and consonant clusters.

Supplement 5: /θ/ *thin* – /s/ *sin*, /θ/ *thin* – /t/ *tin*, /θ/ *thin* – /f/ *fin*

Fact 1. Learners of English sometimes replace the voiceless /θ/ with /s/ (*sank* for *thank*), /t/ (*tank* for *thank*), or /f/ (*free* for *three*).

Fact 2. The voiceless /θ/ occurs in content words (e.g., *think, theory, bath*). The voiced /ð/ occurs primarily in function words (e.g., *the, this, that*) and family relation words (e.g., *mother, brother*).

Listening Activity 1

CD 3; Track 64

Listen to the voiceless *th* /θ/ sound: /θ/ ... /θ/ ... /θ/ ... /θ/ ... /θ/

Listening Activity 2

CD 3; Track 65

Which word in each pair has the /θ/ sound — the first or the second? Close your book and write one or two on a piece of paper.

a. think	sink	**f.** path	pass
b. math	mass	**g.** sought	thought
c. truce	truth	**h.** youth	you
d. three	tree	**i.** tense	tenth
e. mat	math	**j.** thin	fin

Check the answer key. Listen again until you are certain.

Listening Activity 3

CD 3; Track 66

Listen to your teacher, the speaker on audio, or your partner say one of the prompts in each pair. Give the correct response.

PROMPTS (STUDENT 1)	RESPONSES (STUDENT 2)
a. I think it's thin.	(It's not thick.)
I think it's tin.	(It's not aluminum.)
b. She took a bat.	(She wants to play baseball.)
She took a bath.	(She was dirty.)
c. They sent thanks.	(That's thoughtful.)
They sent tanks.	(That's frightening.)

d. I think she'll be three.   (I'm certain she's two now.)

    I think she's free.   (Her calendar looks clear.)

e. Help him. He's sinking.   (He can't swim.)

    Help him. He's thinking.   (He can't solve the problem alone.)

Check the answer key. Or check your answers with your partner.

Listening Activity 4

CD 3; Track 67

Listen to the paragraph. Fill in the blanks with words that have /θ/. Check the answer key.

WHAT MAKES YOU THIN?

What makes you _____? Most people _____ that dieting is the

answer, but researchers say that exercise is the best way to be thin. In one study, _____

men who were not active were put on an exercise program. They walked, jogged, and ran

_____ the one-year program. The first _____ the study showed was that the men

who had exercised the most lost the most weight. The second _____ the study

revealed was that the men who lost the most weight ate more too. The researchers

_____ that fat people don't really eat a lot. Their problem is that they are inactive.

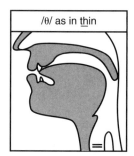

/θ/ as in thin

▲ Forming the voiceless /θ/. Lightly place the tip of the tongue against the cutting edge of the upper teeth. Then direct the air stream through the contact.

Exercise 1

CD 3; Track 68

Repeat these high frequency words with /θ/.

thanks	author	growth
theme	nothing	birth
thin	something	month
thought	anything	south
theory	everything	death
third	method	both

Exercise 2

CD 3; Track 69

Words that contain both /θ/ and /s/, /t/, or /f/ may be especially difficult. Repeat these words.

With /s/	With /t/	With /f/
south	teeth	fourth
something	truth	fifth
thesis	twentieth	faith

Exercise 3

Choose three words with /θ/ that are difficult or that you use frequently. Write a typical phrase or sentence you might say. Practice each sentence three times.

a. _____

b. _____

c. _____

Exercise 4

CD 3; Track 70

Repeat the word pairs in Listening Activity 2.

Exercise 5

CD 3; Track 71

Practice the boldfaced words silently.
Repeat the sentences. Look up from your book as you say each sentence.

a. He was scared to **death**.

b. **Thanks** for coming.

c. According to the **author**, this isn't a serious problem.

d. Is there **anything** else we need to talk about?

e. This **method** isn't very effective.

f. We **both** agreed it was time to do **something**.

g. I **thought** it was **worth** the effort.

Exercise 6

Record yourself reading "What Makes You Thin?" in Listening Activity 4 in the answer key. Monitor the underlined words with /θ/. Then summarize the paragraph in your own words.

Communicative Practice

Practice all words and numbers with /θ/ in the memo. Then imagine that you are a teaching assistant in a North American university. With a partner, take turns announcing the schedule changes using the information in the memo.

MEMORANDUM

TO: All Design Methods 634 Teaching Assistants
SUBJECT: Schedule Change

Please make your students aware of the following changes effective September 20:

	Former Time and place	*New Time and place*
Discussion Section A	Thurs., 8:30 P.M. Classroom Bldg., Room 18	Thurs., 4:30 P.M. Classroom Bldg., Room 23
Discussion Section B	Tues., 2:00 P.M. French Bldg., Room 222	Tues., 2:30 P.M. Thurmond Hall, Room 353

You may also record the announcement. Listen to the recording and circle all the words and numbers with /θ/ that you pronounced *correctly*.

Supplement 6: /f/ *fair* – /p/ *pair*

Fact 1. The /f/ sound is spelled f (<u>f</u>ree), ph (<u>ph</u>ase), and gh (enou<u>gh</u>).

Fact 2. Students sometimes replace the /f/ with /p/ (*copy* for *coffee*).

Listening Activity 1

CD 3; Track 72

Listen to /f/. Notice the friction-like sound as the breath is forced between the upper teeth and inside lower lip: /f/ . . . /f/ . . . /f/ . . . /f/ . . . /f/

Listening Activity 2

CD 3; Track 73

Which word in each pair has the /f/ sound—the first or second? Close your book and write one or two on a piece of paper.

a.	fine	pine	**g.**	fried	pride
b.	coffee	copy	**h.**	cheap	chief
c.	pile	file	**i.**	fill	pill
d.	past	fast	**j.**	past	fast
e.	beef	beep	**k.**	suffer	supper
f.	fashion	passion	**l.**	fact	pact

Check the answer key. Listen again until you are certain.

Listening Activity 3

CD 3; Track 74

Listen to your teacher, the speaker on audio, or your partner say one of the prompts in each pair. Give the correct response.

PROMPTS (STUDENT 1)	RESPONSES (STUDENT 2)
a. It's a new copy machine.	(That's why the copies are so clear.)
It's a new coffee machine.	(That's why the coffee's so good.)
b. It's a fact.	(Do you have proof?)
It's a pact.	(Is everyone in agreement?)
c. He's chief.	(He's the big boss.)
He's cheap.	(We never get raises.)
d. She's driving past.	(Did you see her go by?)
She's driving fast.	(She should slow down.)
e. Excuse me. Where are pans?	(In the houseware department.)
Excuse me. Where are fans?	(In the small appliance department.)

Check the answer key. Or check your answers with your partner.

Listening Activity 4

CD 3; Track 75 Listen to the paragraph. Fill in the blanks with words that have the /f/ sound. Check the answer key.

NEW WORDS AND PHRASES

Each year the American Dialect Society chooses one new word or

_____ of the year. The members usually choose words that

_____ the past year. They _____ words that relate to

current events. For example, in 199__, the phrase of the year was *World Wide Web*. In

1998, the new word was the _____ e- for *electronic*, as in *e-mail*. In 2006,

the word of the year was *plutoed,* a term resulting from the _____ that

Pluto no longer fit the new way planets are _____.

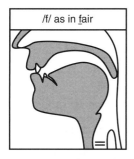

| /f/ as in <u>f</u>air |

▲ Forming the voiceless /f/: Touch the upper front teeth to the inside lower lip. Force air through the light contact.

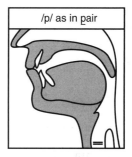

| /p/ as in <u>p</u>air |

▲ Forming the voiceless /p/: Stop the air at the lips. Then release it.

Exercise 1

CD 3; Track 76

Repeat these high frequency words with /f/.

few	affect	proof
function	effective	life
focus	afford	golf
follow	different	half
final	afraid	if
famous	offer	enough
finish	before	himself

Exercise 2

CD 3; Track 77

Words that contain both /f/ and /p/ may be difficult. Repeat these words.

professional, perform, prefer, specify, proof

Consonant clusters with /f/ may also be difficult. Repeat these words.

flat, floor, fly, free, friend, front

lift, left, soft, laughed, gift

Exercise 3

Choose three words with /f/ that are difficult for you or that you use frequently. Write a typical sentence you might say with each of the words. Practice saying each sentence three times.

a. _____

b. _____

c. _____

Exercise 4

Repeat the word pairs in Listening Activity 2.

CD 3; Track 78

Exercise 5

CD 3; Track 79

Practice the boldfaced words silently. Repeat the sentences. Look up from your book as you say each sentence.

a. How're you **feeling**?

b. I'm **fine**.

c. I took quite a **few** notes.

d. Is it close **enough** that we can walk?

e. I'm **afraid** it's too **far**.

f. I'd **prefer** to wait.

g. Does this medication have any side **effects**?

Exercise 6

Record yourself reading "New Words and Phrases" in Listening Activity 4 in the answer key. Monitor your pronunciation of the underlined words with /f/. Then summarize the paragraph in your own words.

Communicative Practice

Complete these superstitions according to beliefs in your country or culture. In groups of five or six, share completed sentences. Which superstitions did you have in common? Can you add another one? Monitor your pronunciation of words with /f/.

1. If you spill salt, . . .

2. If a black cat crosses in **front** of you, . . .

3. If you break a mirror, . . .

4. If you **find** a coin, . . .

5. If a bird **flies** into your house, . . .

6. If you begin a trip on a **Friday**, . . .

7. Add one of your own: _____

Supplement 7: /ʃ/ *sheet* – /s/ *seat*, /ʃ/ *sheet* – /tʃ/ *cheat*

Fact 1. The /ʃ/ is most commonly spelled *sh* (*she*) and *-ti-* (*nation*), but it is also spelled *-ci-* (*social*), *-ssi-* (*discussion*), and *-ssu-* (*issue*).

Fact 2. Some students replace /ʃ/ with /s/ (*see* for *she*). Others replace /ʃ/ with /tʃ/ (*chair* for *share* or vice versa).

Listening Activity 1

CD 4; Track 1

Listen to the /ʃ/ and notice the continuous release of breath:
/ʃ/ . . . /ʃ/ . . . /ʃ/ . . . /ʃ/ . . . /ʃ/

Listening Activity 2

CD 4; Track 2

Which word in each pair has the /ʃ/ sound—the first or the second? Close your book and write one or two on a piece of paper.

a. sheet	seat		**f.** sore	shore
b. shoes	choose		**g.** shore	chore
c. see	she		**h.** watching	washing
d. sheet	cheat		**i.** sour	shower
e. chop	shop		**j.** catch	cash

Check the answer key. Listen again until you are certain.

Listening Activity 3

CD 4; Track 3

Listen to your teacher, the speaker on audio, or your partner say one of the prompts in each pair. Give the correct response.

PROMPTS (STUDENT 1)	RESPONSES (STUDENT 2)
a. What's he washing?	(His sheets.)
What's he watching?	(A football game.)
b. It's going to shower.	(Is rain predicted?)
It's going to sour.	(Should I put it in the refrigerator?)
c. Can you catch this?	(Sure. I used to play baseball.)
Can you cash this?	(Sure. I'm going to the bank.)
d. She feels the shame.	(Although she wasn't responsible.)
She feels the same.	(She's in complete agreement.)

Check the answer key. Or check your answers with your partner.

Listening Activity 4

CD 4; Track 4

Listen to the following paragraph. Fill in the blanks with words that have the /ʃ/ sound. Check the answer key.

SHYNESS

About 92 million Americans are _____. Researchers are taking an interest in shyness and have reached different conclusions. According to one study, _____ relations nowadays are more complex, and shyness is becoming a _____ concern. Another study found that only about half of the shy people were tense in _____ situations, contrary to popular belief. And still another study found that shy people tend to be more stable in their _____. Some psychologists think that shyness may be inherited, whereas others think that shyness is cultural.

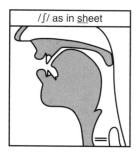

/ʃ/ as in sheet

▲ Forming the voiceless /ʃ/: Raise the front part of the tongue toward the hard palate. Press the sides of the tongue against the teeth. Force air over the tongue. (Or start from /s/ and pull your tongue back and up.)

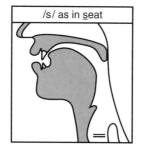

/s/ as in seat

▲ Forming the voiceless /s/: Raise the front part of the tongue toward the **front** of the hard palate. Press the sides of the tongue against the teeth, forming a valley down the center of the tongue. Force air through the valley, making a hissing sound.

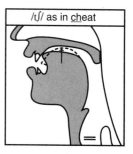

/tʃ/ as in cheat

▲ Forming the voiceless /tʃ/: Make a /t/ then an /ʃ/ sound. First, press the tongue against the gum ridge to stop the air. Then release the tip of the tongue as you say /ʃ/.

Exercise 1

CD 4; Track 5

Repeat these high-frequency words with /ʃ/.

she	issue	wish
shut	special	wash
should	social	push
shoulder	financial	publish
shop	especially	establish
short	initial	finish
shout	ensure	fresh

Exercise 2

CD 4; Track 6

Words that contain both /ʃ/ and /s/ or /tʃ/ are especially difficult. Repeat these words.

situation, selfish, social, section, special, insurance

Exercise 3

Choose three words with /ʃ/ that are difficult or that you use frequently. Write a typical phrase or sentence you might say with the words. Practice each sentence three times.

a. _____

b. _____

c. _____

Exercise 4

CD 4; Track 7

Repeat the word pairs in Listening Activity 2.

Exercise 5

CD 4; Track 8

Practice the boldfaced words silently.
Repeat the sentences. Look up from your book as you say each sentence.

a. You can get some **cash** at the ATM.

b. Why isn't he doing his **share**?

c. Teachers are under a lot of **pressure** to give more tests.

d. They're trying to **establish** a more stable government.

e. She's fluent in **English** and **Spanish**.

f. You'll have to **push** them to get the work **finished**.

g. Excuse me. Are the **shrimp fresh**?

Exercise 6

Record yourself reading "Shyness" in Listening Activity 4 in the answer key. Monitor your pronunciation of the underlined words with /ʃ/. Then summarize the paragraph in your own words.

Communicative Practice 1

In small groups of three to five students, compare and contrast the university systems in your countries. Monitor your pronunciation of /ʃ/ in key terms during your discussion. Share highlights of your group's discussion with the class.

USEFUL VOCABULARY WITH /ʃ/	TOPICS FOR DISCUSSION
discussion participation	**a.** The interaction between the students and professors in the classroom.
relationship friendship professional	**b.** Relationships among students and professors outside the classroom.
scholarships financial tuition	**c.** Costs per year; financial aid.
admission competition pressure applications	**d.** Criteria for admission.

Communicative Practice 2

With a small group, create nutritious lunch and dinner menus containing foods that have the /ʃ/ and /tʃ/ sounds (e.g., boiled shrimp, grilled chicken, steamed squash, etc.)

Supplement 8: /r/ *right* – /l/ *light*, /r/ *grad* – /l/ *glad*

Fact 1. The /r/ sound is usually spelled *r* (<u>r</u>oad); /r/ is occasionally spelled *wr* (<u>wr</u>ong).

Fact 2. Some students replace /r/ with /l/ (*collect* for *correct*) or /r/ with /w/ (*west* for *rest*). Other students make /r/ by tapping the tongue against the upper gum ridge. The tongue-tap /r/ is not as likely to cause misunderstanding.

Something to Think About

If you use a tongue tap /r/, that is, an /r/ that sounds like a quick /d/, here a few words that might be misunderstood.

wearing	*might sound like*	wedding or wetting
hiring	*might sound like*	hiding
earring	*might sound like*	eating
firing	*might sound like*	fighting
hearing	*might sound like*	heating or heeding

If you frequently use any of these words with American English speakers, say them with a North American English /r/ to avoid misunderstanding.

Listening Activity 1

Listen to the /r/ sound: /r/ . . . /r/ . . . /r/ . . . /r/ . . . /r/

CD 4; Track 9

Listening Activity 2

Which word of each pair has the /r/ sound—the first or the second? Close your book and write one or two on a piece of paper.

CD 4; Track 10

a. late	rate	**f.** run	one	**k.** appeal	appear
b. wrong	long	**g.** went	rent	**l.** firing	filing
c. leader	reader	**h.** low	row	**m.** grad	glad
d. rock	lock	**i.** red	led	**n.** free	fee
e. write	light	**j.** flight	fright	**o.** pay	pray

Check the answer key. Listen again until you are certain.

Listening Activity 3

Listen to your teacher, the speaker on audio, or your partner say one of the prompts in each pair. Give the correct response.

CD 4; Track 11

PROMPTS (STUDENT 1)	RESPONSES (STUDENT 2)
a. You have the long number.	(You need the short one.)
You have the wrong number.	(Hang up and dial again.)
b. Where do they pray?	(At the mosque.)
Where do they play?	(At the playground.)
c. I watched the clouds go by.	(In the sky.)
I watched the crowds go by.	(In the street.)
d. He's learning to lead.	(As a manager.)
He's learning to read.	(In first grade.)
e. They're grad students.	(Not undergrad.)
They're glad students.	(Not sad.)
f. That's where all of the fat guys live.	(Oh, you must mean *frat* guys.)
That's where all the frat guys live.	(So that's fraternity row.)

Check the answer key. Or check your answers with your partner.

Listening Activity 4

Listen to the paragraph. Fill in the blanks with words that have the /r/ sound. Check the answer key.

CD 4; Track 12

BUTTERFLIES IN YOUR STOMACH

If you've ever given a _____ in front of a class or a group of people, you know the feeling. Your heart _____, your blood pressure _____, your hands start to shake, your throat gets _____, and you get butterflies in your stomach. What causes your body to _____ this way? When you are nervous, your glands _____ adrenaline into your bloodstream. The adrenaline causes your muscles to tense up. It also causes increased motion in your stomach muscles. As a _____, your stomach _____ more acid than it needs for digestion. The acid feels like butterflies in your stomach.

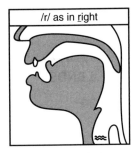

/r/ as in right

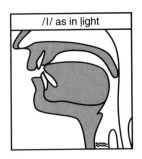

/l/ as in light

▲ Forming the voiced /r/ sound: Turn the tip of the tongue up, but do not touch the palate. The sides of the tongue touch the back teeth. Lips may be slightly rounded.

▲ Forming the voiced /l/ sound: Imagine holding a piece of candy on the gum ridge with the very tip of the tongue. The air flows around the sides of the tongue.

A Helpful Hint

If you feel the tip of your tongue touching something, you are probably saying /l/, not /r/.

Exercise 1

CD 4; Track 13

Repeat these words with the /r/ sound.

INITIAL	MIDDLE	BLENDS
rather	correct	grow
write	married	graduate
room	parents	crime
wrong	sorry	crowd
ready	pirate	fruit
reason	arrive	free
rest	tomorrow	price
repeat	carry	prove
rice	hearing	drive
research	firing	program

Exercise 2

CD 4; Track 14

Words that contain both an /r/ and an /l/ may be especially difficult. Repeat these words.

really, realize, relation, library, relief, rely, religion, problem, salary, frequently, parallel

Exercise 3

Choose three words with /r/ that are difficult or that you use frequently. Write a typical phrase or sentence you might say with each of the words. Practice each sentence three times.

a. _____

b. _____

c. _____

Exercise 4

CD 4; Track 15

Repeat the word pairs in Listening Activity 2.

Exercise 5

Practice the boldfaced words silently.

CD 4; Track 16   Repeat the sentences. Look up from your book as you say each sentence.

a. Turn **right** at the next light.
b. That bumper sticker says, **Arrive** Alive!
c. He'd like to be **rich** enough to **travel**.

d. Are gas **prices** still **increasing**?

e. I'm not quite **ready** to leave.

f. I stopped by to check on your **progress**.

g. Who's the lead in the **research project**?

h. I'd **rather** have **rice**.

Exercise 6

Record yourself reading the paragraph titled "Butterflies in Your Stomach" in Listening Activity 4 in the answer key. Monitor your pronunciation of underlined words with /r/. Then summarize the paragraph in your own words.

Communicative Practice

In a group of three or four students, underline and practice the pronunciation of menu items with an /r/ sound.

Student 1 is the server and writes down what each customer wants. Student 1 has descriptions of the menu items on next page. The other students are customers and order complete meals. If customers want explanations of the entrees, they should ask the server and not look at the next page.

MENU

Entrees

Served with your choice of two vegetables, a garden salad with choice of dressing, and rolls

Pasta Primavera	Meat Loaf	Leg of Lamb
Southern Fried Chicken	Chicken Teriyaki	Fried Calamari
London Broil	Crabmeat au Gratin	Burritos

Today's Special

Broiled Flounder Fillets
Served with brown rice, fresh peas, and crusty French bread

Vegetables

French-fried potatoes
Sliced tomatoes with basil
Broccoli spears
Zucchini-carrot medley
Stir-fried vegetables
French-style green beans

Beverages

Fresh brewed coffee
Tea—hot or iced
Soft drinks
Milk
Lemonade

Desserts

Fresh fruit sorbet—assorted flavors
Blueberry pie a la mode
Carrot cake

Fresh strawberries in season
Hot fudge ice-cream sundae

Pasta Primavera

Ribbons of fettuccini and fresh vegetables tossed in a yogurt sauce, sprinkled with Parmesan cheese

Southern Fried Chicken

Fried to a crispy golden brown

London Broil

Grilled strips of flank steak served with fresh mushrooms

Choice of Salad Dressings:

House Dressing—Vinaigrette
Ranch
Blue Cheese
French

Meat Loaf

Low-fat; made with lean ground beef

Chicken Teriyaki

Grilled strips of chicken marinated in spicy teriyaki sauce

Crabmeat au Gratin

Crabmeat in a creamy cheese sauce, baked to a delicate brown

Leg of Lamb

Marinated in red wine and rosemary

Fried Calamari

Fried in a light batter

Burritos

Your choice of beef, chicken, or beans; served with rice and fresh salsa

Beyond the Pronunciation Classroom: Eating Out

Bring menus from nearby restaurants to class. Compare dishes and prices. Practice ordering dishes with /r/ and /l/. Make plans to go to lunch together.

Supplement 9: /v/ *very* – /w/ *wary*, /v/ *very* – /b/ *berry*

Fact. Some students replace the /v/ with a /w/ (*wheel* for *veal* and vice versa). Other students replace the /v/ with a /b/ (*berry* for *very*).

Listening Activity 1

CD 4; Track 17

Listen to the /v/ sound: /v/ ... /v/ ... /v/ ... /v/ ... /v/

Listening Activity 2

CD 4; Track 18

Which word in each pair has the /v/ sound—the first or the second? Close your book and write one or two on a piece of paper.

a. very	wary		**h.** vow	wow
b. very	where he		**i.** vie	why
c. west	vest		**j.** boats	votes
d. veil	whale		**k.** ban	van
e. wheel	veal		**l.** vary	berry
f. verse	worse		**m.** have it	habit
g. evoke	awoke			

EAP 0485

Check the answer key. Listen again until you are certain.

Listening Activity 3

CD 4; Track 19

Listen to your teacher, the speaker on audio, or your partner say one of the prompts in each pair. Give the correct response.

PROMPTS (STUDENT 1)	RESPONSES (STUDENT 2)
a. Where did you put the veal?	(In the freezer.)
Where did you put the wheel?	(On the bike.)
b. What kind of wine did you get?	(A white cooking wine.)
What kind of vine did you get?	(One with blue flowers.)
c. They evoke her.	(They remind me of her.)
They awoke her.	(They didn't want her to oversleep.)
d. What happened with the vote?	(Our candidate won.)
What happened with the boat?	(The engine died.)
e. Are they moving again?	(Our neighbors?)
Are they mooing again?	(The cows?)

Check the answer key. Or check your answers with your partner.

Listening Activity 4

CD 4; Track 20

Listen to the paragraph. Fill in the blanks with words that have the /v/ sound. Check the answer key.

VALENTINE'S DAY

All _____ the world, it is popular to _____ cards, flowers, gifts, and other tokens of _____ on February 14, St. Valentine's Day. There are _____ explanations for the origin of this holiday; _____, the most believable is that St. Valentine's Day is a _____ of a February 15th Roman _____. During this festival, bachelors picked names of women to _____ who their "valentines" would be for the coming year. The couples then exchanged gifts and sometimes even became engaged.

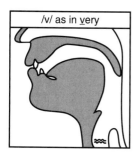

/v/ as in very

▲ Forming the voiced /v/ sound: Lightly touch the upper teeth to the inside of the lower lip. Force air through the contact. Voice the sound.

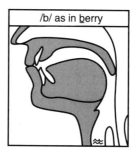

/b/ as in berry

▲ Forming the voiced /b/ sound: Stop the air stream at the lips. Then release it.
Note: To say the voiced /w/, lips are tightly rounded.

Exercise 1

CD 4; Track 21

Repeat these words with /v/.

vote	level	achieve
view	never	believe
voice	over	leave
visit	prevent	move
vital	favor	love
very	driver	serve
variety	develop	alive
volume	division	save
vacation	avoid	you've
version	individual	improve

Exercise 2

CD 4; Track 22

Words with /v/ and /w/, /b/, or /f/ may be especially difficult. Repeat these words.

With /w/	With /b/	With /f/
vowel	behavior	forgive
wives	observe	favor
we've	believe	fever

Exercise 3

Choose three words with /v/ that are difficult or that you use frequently. Write a typical phrase or sentence you might say with each of the words. Practice each sentence three times.

a. _____

b. _____

c. _____

Exercise 4

CD 4; Track 23

Repeat the word pairs in Listening Activity 2.

Exercise 5

CD 4; Track 24

Practice the boldfaced words silently.
Repeat the sentences. Look up from the book as you say each sentence.

a. Could you do me a **favor**?

b. Where did you go on your **vacation**?

c. Which **movie** did you see?

d. Maybe I should take his **advice**.

e. He can't hear the **TV** at a normal **volume**.

f. He **never** bothers to tell us where he's going.

g. She has a **lovely** accent.

h. The watch isn't worth much, but it has sentimental **value**.

i. We'll do **everything** we can to **prevent** any more damage.

Exercise 6

Record yourself reading *Valentine's Day* in Listening Activity 4 in the answer key. Monitor the underlined words with /v/. Then summarize the paragraph in your own words.

Communicative Practice

In a group of three to five students, discuss vacation time in your countries. Monitor for the /v/ sound in the key vocabulary listed below. Be careful to use /w/, not /v/, in these words: worker, white-collar, one, and week. Report the highlights of your discussion to the class.

USEFUL VOCABULARY WITH /v/	SUGGESTED TOPICS FOR DISCUSSION
*v*aries ha*v*e a*v*erage	**a.** How long is the a*v*erage *v*acation for blue-collar workers in your country?
se*v*en e*v*ery *v*acation fi*v*e	**b.** How long is the a*v*erage *v*acation for white-collar workers in your country?

ser*v*ice
deser*v*e

c. What is the relationship between length of ser*v*ice in a company and length of *v*acation? Do workers in your country usually take all of the vacation they deser*v*e?

go*v*ernment

d. Do any laws in your country go*v*ern *v*acation time?

tra*v*el
*v*isit
o*v*erseas
dri*v*e

e. How do people in your country like to spend their *v*acations?

Prime-Time Practice

Investigate local volunteer opportunities on the Internet or in the newspaper. Report two or three of the most interesting opportunities back to your small group or to the class.

Vowel Supplements

Supplement 10: Front, Central, Back Vowels, and Diphthongs

This section introduces the fifteen North American English vowel sounds and their phonetic symbols. The vowel sounds of American English are classified as front or back and high or low.

Exercise 1

1. Put your finger on your upper lip. Compare /iʸ/ as in *me* with /uʷ/ as in *you*: What happens?

With front vowels like /iʸ/, the lips are _____.

With back vowels like /uʷ/, the lips are _____.

2. Put your finger on your chin. Compare /iʸ/ as in *me* with /ɑ/ as in *f<u>a</u>ther*. What happens?

With high vowels like /iʸ/, the jaw (and tongue) are _____.

With low vowels like /ɑ/, the jaw (and tongue) are _____.
Then, check the answer key.

Front Vowels

Front vowels are made with the front of the tongue arched. Beginning with the highest front vowel /iʸ/, the front of the tongue is high in the mouth. The tongue and jaw drop as you say the rest of the front vowels. Front vowels are made with the lips spread.

Exercise 2

CD 4; Track 25

Repeat the front vowel sounds and the key words after your teacher or the speaker on audio.

Vowel 1. /iʸ/   h**e**, f**ee**t, m**ea**t

Vowel 2. /ɪ/   h**i**t, **i**f, p**i**ck

Vowel 3. /eʸ/   m**ay**, **A**sia, f**a**ce, p**ai**n

Vowel 4. /ɛ/   l**e**t, h**ea**d, w**e**ll

Vowel 5. /æ/   m**a**d, **a**sk, c**a**sh

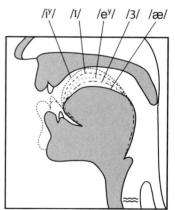
/iʸ/ /ɪ/ /eʸ/ /ɜ/ /æ/

▲ The tongue positions for front vowels

185

Central Vowels

 Central vowels are made with the *middle* of the tongue slightly arched. The tongue and jaw are higher for /ʌ/ and /ə/ than for /ɑ/. The lips are neither spread nor rounded. They are in a neutral position.

Exercise 3

 Repeat the central vowel sounds and key words after your teacher or the speaker on audio.

CD 4; Track 26

Vowel 6.*	/ɜr/	g**ir**l, t**ur**n, le**ar**n
	/ər/	bett**er**, eff**or**t
Vowel 7.*	/ʌ/	c**u**t, **u**p, f**u**nny
	/ə/	**a**bout, c**o**ncern
Vowel 8.	/ɑ/	c**o**ncert, f**a**ther

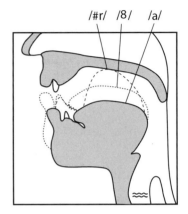

▲ The tongue positions for central vowels

Back Vowels

 Back vowels are made with the *back* part of the tongue arched. Beginning with the highest back vowel /uʷ/, the back part of the tongue is high. The tongue and jaw drop lower as you say the rest of the back vowels. Back vowels are made with the lips more or less rounded.

Exercise 4

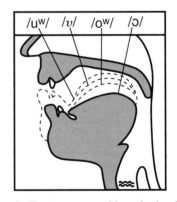 Repeat the back vowel sounds and the key words after your teacher or the speaker on audio.

CD 4; Track 27

Vowel 9.	/uʷ/	too, food, rude, flew, juice
Vowel 10.	/ʊ/	took, foot, should, put
Vowel 11.	/oʷ/	no, low, hope, loan
Vowel 12.	/ɔ/	law, cause

Note: Some speakers of American English do not distinguish between /ɑ/ as in c*o*t and /ɔ/ as in c*au*ght.

▲ The tongue positions for back vowels

Diphthongs

 Diphthongs combine two vowel sounds. Your mouth moves from the first sound to the second sound. Diphthongs have two symbols—one symbol for each sound.

*Vowels 6 and 7 have two symbols. The /ɜr/ and /ʌ/ are used in stressed content words and stressed syllables. The /ər/ and /ə/ are used in unstressed function words (e.g., "I'll give h**er** a call") and in unstressed syllables (e.g., **a**lone).

Exercise 5

Repeat these three diphthongs and the key words after your teacher or the speaker on audio.

Vowel 13. /aɪ/ tie, like, by

Vowel 14. /aʊ/ out, loud, now

Vowel 15. /ɔɪ/ toy, voice

Note: Four vowel sounds—/iʸ/, /eʸ/, /uʷ/, and /oʷ/ — are like diphthongs, but they are not true diphthongs. These sounds glide toward a second sound, but the second sound is not complete. That is why the second symbol is smaller.

Supplement 11: Phonetic Alphabet and Vowel Chart

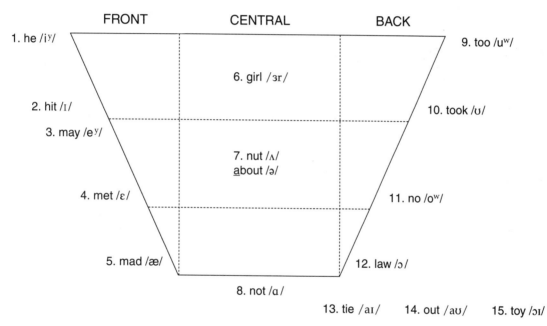

▲ The vowel chart with the 15 vowel sounds of North American English.

1. Look at the vowel chart, and circle sounds that you do not have in your first language.

2. List any vowel sounds that are difficult for you. You can refer to your *Speech Profile Form* in Chapter 1.

_____ _____ _____ _____

Follow-up: This Web site shows you how to pronounce the vowel sounds of English. www.uiowa.edu/~acadtech/phonetics/english/frameset.html. Locate the vowel you want to practice. Put a small mirror next to the computer screen so that you can see yourself. Imitate the speaker's mouth positions.

Supplement 12: Tense and Lax Vowels

 The vowels /iʸ/ in *he*, /eʸ/ in *made*, /uʷ/ in *too*, /oʷ/ in *know*, /ɑ/ in *hot*, and /ɔ/ in *law* are *tense* and pronounced with muscle tension. They are longer in duration. The remaining vowels are shorter in duration and are made with the muscles in a more relaxed or *lax* position.

Exercise 1

CD 4; Track 29

Hearing and saying the difference between tense and lax vowels is difficult for many students.
Repeat the sounds and words. Notice your face and tongue muscles tense and relax.

TENSE	LAX
/iʸ/ he	/ɪ/ hit
/eʸ/ made	/ɛ/ met
/uʷ/ too	/ʊ/ took
/ɑ/ lock	/ʌ/ luck

A Helpful Hint

 If you have trouble hearing the difference between two vowel sounds, ask a proficient English speaker to whisper the vowels. You might be able to distinguish the two sounds more easily.

Exercise 2

Listen as your teacher whispers the tense and lax sound pairs below.

TENSE	LAX
a. /iʸ/ he	/ɪ/ hit
b. /eʸ/ made	/ɛ/ met
c. /uʷ/ too	/ʊ/ took

Was it easier for you to hear the difference between the whispered sounds? Now your teacher will whisper a tense or lax vowel or word in each pair. Hold up one finger for tense or two fingers for lax.

Exercise 3

Watch your teacher *mime* the sound pairs. Notice the mouth movement toward a second sound in the tense vowels. Notice the pure quality of the lax vowels.

TENSE	LAX
a. /iʸ/ he	/ɪ/ hit
b. /eʸ/ made	/ɛ/ met
c. /uʷ/ too	/ʊ/ took
d. /oʷ/ coat	/ʌ/ cut

This next section provides concentrated practice with vowel sounds that continue to be troublesome for many intermediate to advanced speakers of English.

Something to Think About

As you study vowel sounds, remember to use good stress and rhythm. The most important vowel sounds in an utterance are those in key words and syllables, that is, the words and syllables with the most emphasis.

Supplement 13: /ɪ/ *fit* – /iʸ/ *feet*

Fact 1. The /ɪ/ is a pure vowel; it is short in duration. The /iʸ/ is a little longer and may glide slightly higher.

Fact 2. Many students confuse /ɪ/ and /iʸ/ and say *feet* for *fit* or vice versa.

Listening Activity 1

CD 4; Track 30

Listen to /ɪ/: /ɪ/ . . . /ɪ/ . . . /ɪ/ . . . /ɪ/

Now listen to /ɪ/ contrasted with /iʸ/: /ɪ/ . . . /iʸ/ . . . /ɪ/ . . . /iʸ/ . . . /ɪ/ . . . /iʸ/

Listening Activity 2

CD 4; Track 31

Listen to words with /ɪ/: *disk, give, miss, rich, city, minute, live, consider, visit, issue*

Listening Activity 3

CD 4; Track 32

Which word in each pair has the /ɪ/ sound—the first or the second? Close your book and write one or two on a separate piece of paper.

a. hit	heat	**f.** live	leave
b. it	eat	**g.** seen	sin
c. heel	hill	**h.** list	least
d. cheap	chip	**i.** will	wheel
e. feet	fit	**j.** sleep	slip

Check the answer key. Listen again until you are certain.

Listening Activity 4

CD 4; Track 33

Listen to your teacher, the speaker on audio, or your partner say one of the prompts in each pair. Give the correct response.

PROMPTS (STUDENT 1)	RESPONSES (STUDENT 2)
a. Did you slip?	(Yeah! On that ice.)
Did you sleep?	(Yeah! For 10 hours.)
b. Those were beautiful pitches.	(It was a great game.)
Those were beautiful peaches.	(It was a good crop.)
c. Is the patient going to live?	(Yes. He's in good condition.)
Is the patient going to leave?	(Yes. She's packing her bags.)
d. Did you hit it?	(Yes, with the hammer.)
Did you heat it?	(Yes, in the microwave.)
e. Where should I put these pills?	(In the medicine cabinet.)
Where should I put these peels?	(In the garbage can.)

Check the answer key. Or check your answers with your partner.

Listening Activity 5

CD 4; Track 34

Listen to the following paragraph. Fill in the blanks with the words that have the /ɪ/ sound in stressed words and syllables. Check the answer key.

DRINKING AND HEALTH RISKS

People often _____ a glass to toast good health. Drinking may indeed lower the _____ of several diseases, according to _____ released by the Harvard School of Public Health. Researchers found that one to two _____ each day reduced the risk of heart disease by about twenty-_____ percent in men and up to _____ percent in women. Researchers warn, however, that drinking can increase other health risks. Alcohol is _____ to a higher risk of breast cancer in women and to a higher rate of _____disease.

Source: www.med.unc.edu.

Exercise 1

CD 4; Track 35

Repeat the words with /ɪ/.

*i*ssue	live
*i*ncrease, (*n.*)	l*i*mit
*i*ncome	link
*i*mpact	lift
*i*mmigrate	l*i*sten
*i*ntegrate	k*i*tchen
*i*nfluence	cons*i*der
*i*nterview	comm*i*ttee
*i*nterested	cond*i*tion

Exercise 2

CD 4; Track 36

Repeat the word pairs in Listening Activity 3.

Exercise 3

Choose three words with /ɪ/ that you use frequently. Write typical sentences you might say with the words. Practice each sentence three times.

a. _____

b. _____

c. _____

Exercise 4

Practice the words with boldfaced letters silently.
Repeat the sentences. Look up from your book as you say each sentence.

CD 4; Track 37

a. The doctor has to take my medical history.

b. Lunch will be about six dollars.

c. I don't know. What do *you* think?

d. Put the fish and chicken in the freezer.

e. There's a limit of one per person.

f. I live in the fifth house on the right.

g. It'll take four people to lift this table.

h. Let's hurry! We're going to miss the beginning.

Exercise 5

Record yourself reading *Drinking and Health Risks* in Listening Activity 5 in the answer key. Monitor your pronunciation of the underlined words with /ɪ/. Summarize the paragraph in your own words.

Communicative Practice

Practice the /ɪ/ sound as you create a "wish list." Pick five items that would most improve the quality of life. Number them in order of importance. Then, practice these words with /ɪ/ that are likely to occur during the discussion: *if, think, wish, oPInion, pick, list, indiVIdual,* and *fifth.*

In small groups, discuss the items most important to you. Try to reach consensus on the top two items.

WISH LIST

INDIVIDUAL	GROUP	
_____	_____	Quality education for everyone
_____	_____	Four-day work week
_____	_____	Drug-free world
_____	_____	Human colonies in space
_____	_____	Personal robots
_____	_____	End to prejudice
_____	_____	Housing for the homeless

——	——	Cures for deadly diseases
——	——	Adequate health care for everyone
——	——	Ban on personal weapons
——	——	Full employment
——	——	End to hunger
——	——	Nonpolluting energy sources

Supplement 14: /ɛ/ *pen* – /eʸ/ *pain*, /ɛ/ *pen* – /æ/ *pan*

Fact 1. The /ɛ/ and /æ/ are pure vowels; they are short in duration. The /eʸ/ is longer in duration and glides upward.

Fact 2. Many students replace the /ɛ/ with /eʸ/ (*late* for *let*) and vice versa. Other students may use /ɛ/ for the /æ/ sound (*bed* for *bad*).

Listening Activity 1

Listen to /ɛ/: /ɛ/ ... /ɛ/ ... /ɛ/ ... /ɛ/

CD 4; Track 38 Now listen to the contrast between /ɛ/ and /eʸ/: /ɛ/ ... /eʸ/ ... /ɛ/ ... /eʸ/ ... /ɛ/ ... /eʸ/

Listening Activity 2

Listen to the words with /ɛ/: *let, yes, end, dead, met, left, guess, better, never, effective*

CD 4; Track 39

Listening Activity 3

Does the first or the second word in each pair have the /ɛ/ sound? Close your book and write one or two on a piece of paper.

CD 4; Track 40

a. late	let	**e.** taste	test	**i.** guess	gas		
b. date	debt	**f.** men	main	**j.** men	man		
c. wet	weight	**g.** fell	fail	**k.** taxes	Texas		
d. edge	age	**h.** later	letter	**l.** celery	salary		

Check the answer key.

Listening Activity 4

CD 4; Track 41

Listen to your teacher, the speaker on audio, or your partner say one of the prompts in each pair. Give the correct response.

PROMPTS (STUDENT 1)	RESPONSES (STUDENT 2)
a. Could you get some black pepper?	(For dinner.)
Could you get some black paper?	(For my art project.)
b. He just left.	(Sorry you missed him.)
He just laughed.	(He thought it was funny.)
c. How did you like the test?	(It was really hard.)
How did you like the taste?	(Too spicy.)
d. I met the men you work with.	(Did you like them?)
I met the man you work with.	(Did you like him?)
e. It's the right edge.	(Good and sharp.)
It's the right age.	(Not too old and not too young.)

Check the answer key. Or check the answers with your partner.

Listening Activity 5

CD 4; Track 42

Listen to the following paragraph. Fill in the blanks with words that have the /ɛ/ sound in stressed words and syllables. Check the answer key.

AIRBAGS

Airbags have become standard equipment in new cars. They are stored in the

_____ of the steering wheel, in the instrument panel, in the doors, and

sometimes in the roof. In an accident, they quickly inflate to _____ save lives.

But how do they work? Airbags have electronic _____ that can feel a crash as

it begins to happen. The sensors _____ off a gas that rushes into the bags.

The soft bags _____ the people in the car and _____ the bags deflate.

Exercise 1

CD 4; Track 43

Repeat the words with /ɛ/.

*e*nd	*e*mpty	m*e*t	n*e*ver
*a*ny	*e*ffort	test	cr*e*dit
*e*xtra	*e*nsure	let	sp*e*cify
*e*xit	*e*nter	g*ue*ss	perc*e*nt

Exercise 2

Repeat the word pairs in Listening Activity 3.

Exercise 3

Choose three words with /ɛ/ that you use frequently. Write typical sentences you might say with the words. Practice each sentence three times.

a. _____

b. _____

c. _____

Exercise 4

Practice the words with boldfaced letters silently.

Repeat the sentences. Look up from your book as you say the sentences.

a. My relatives left yesterday.

b. That was an excellent question.

c. Did you forget to send the letter?

d. The election is in November.

e. My best friend sent this to me.

f. I've already spent everything that you lent me.

g. Take the elevator to the second floor.

h. The recipe calls for a teaspoon of black pepper.

Exercise 5

Record yourself reading *Airbags* in Listening Activity 5 in the answer key. Monitor your pronunciation of the underlined words with /ɛ/. Be sure to use /eʸ/ in the words *save, inflate,* and *deflate.* Then summarize the paragraph in your own words.

Communicative Practice

Look at the list of qualities in the box below. What is the sound of the stressed or bold vowels in the words below? Write the words in the correct columns. The first one has been done.

ethical	wealthy	faithful	generous
stable	patient	entertaining	sensitive
sense of humor	healthy	intelligent	*Other:* _____

/ɛ/ as in *pen*   /eʸ/ as in *pain*

ethical _____   _____

_____   _____

_____   _____

_____   _____

_____

_____

In a small group, compare the top two or three qualities you would seek in a friend and the top two or three qualities you would seek in a spouse.

Friend: _____ _____ _____

Spouse: _____ _____ _____

Discuss how the qualities differ.

Supplement 15: /ʌ/ *luck* – /ɑ/ *lock*

Fact 1. The /ʌ/ is a central vowel. The tongue and lips are relaxed. The lips are neither rounded nor spread.

Fact 2. Many students confuse /ʌ/ with /ɑ/ so that *shot* sounds like *shut* and vice-versa.

Listening Activity 1

Listen to the /ʌ/ sound: /ʌ/ ... /ʌ/ ... /ʌ/ ... /ʌ/

CD 4; Track 46

Listen to /ʌ/ contrasted with /ɑ/: /ʌ/ ... /ɑ/ ... /ʌ/ ... /ɑ/ ... /ʌ/ ... /ɑ/

Listening Activity 2

Listen to the words with /ʌ/: *up, sun, cut, luck, trust, run, study, public, love, number, money*

CD 4; Track 47

Listening Activity 3

CD 4; Track 48

Does the first or the second word in each pair have the /ʌ/ sound? Close your book and write one or two on a separate piece of paper.

a. lock	luck	**e.** shut	shot
b. box	bucks	**f.** robber baron	rubber baron
c. dug	dog	**g.** color	collar
d. fund	fond	**h.** duck	dock

Check the answer key.

Listening Activity 4

CD 4; Track 49

Listen to your teacher, the speaker on audio, or your partner say one of the prompts in each pair. Give the correct response.

PROMPTS (STUDENT 1)	RESPONSES (STUDENT 2)
a. Is that a duck?	(Yes. It has feathers.)
Is that a dog?	(Yes. It has fur.)
b. I need a cup.	(For coffee.)
I need a cop.	(To report an accident.)
c. What an ugly collar.	(I hate buttons on collars.)
What an ugly color.	(I hate that shade of green.)
d. This is a hard nut.	(I can't crack it.)
This is a hard knot.	(I can't untie it.)
e. Was your luck good?	(No. I lost.)
Was your lock good?	(No. It broke.)

Check the answer key. Or check your answers with your partner.

Listening Activity 5

CD 4; Track 50

Listen to the following paragraph. Fill in the blanks with words that have the /ʌ/ sound in stressed words and syllables. Check the answer key.

NUMBERS OF FOREIGN-BORN ARE UP IN U.S.

Based on the results of a _____ in 2002, the Census Bureau reported that more than _____ in every 10 residents of the United States was foreign-born. The number was more than _____ the percentage of foreign born in 1970 (4.8 percent). _____ of the foreign-born population — almost one third — resides in California. New York ranks second and Florida third. The government study also includes where immigrants are_____. One of every two foreign-born residents _____ from Central and South America and the Caribbean.

Source: U.S. Census Bureau.

Exercise 1

CD 4; Track 51

Repeat words with /ʌ/.

up	m**u**ch
under	j**u**st
uncle	cl**u**b
ultimately	l**u**nch
upper	n**u**mber
update	b**u**s
upkeep	bl**oo**d
upturn	s**u**mmary

Exercise 2

CD 4; Track 52

Repeat the word pairs in Listening Activity 3.

Exercise 3

Choose three words with /ʌ/ that you use frequently. Write typical sentences you might say with the words. Practice each sentence three times.

a. _____

b. _____

c. _____

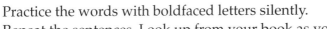

Exercise 4

Practice the words with boldfaced letters silently.
Repeat the sentences. Look up from your book as you say each sentence.

CD 4; Track 53

a. Let's disc**u**ss these ass**u**mptions.

b. Do you have en**ou**gh money for l**u**nch?

c. Are you going to st**u**dy this s**u**mmer?

d. We have an**o**ther meeting on M**o**nday?

e. I w**o**nder what we're having for s**u**pper.

f. He sent a d**o**zen roses to his m**o**ther.

g. He gave the speaker a short introd**u**ction.

h. X is a f**u**nction of y.

Exercise 5

Record yourself reading *Numbers of Foreign-Born Are Up in U.S.* in Listening Activity 5 in the answer key. Monitor your pronunciation of the underlined words with /ʌ/.

Communicative Practice

Whom do you trust? Each year the Gallup Poll asks people in the U.S. to rank professions for "honesty and ethical standards." How would *you* rank these professions? Write the professions in order from most to least trusted.

PROFESSIONS

senators	lawyers	bankers
dentists	veterinarians	college teachers
pharmacists	police officers	state governors
nurses	business executives	insurance salespeople

RANK

Most Trusted

1. _____
2. _____
3. _____
4. _____
5. _____
6. _____
7. _____
8. _____
9. _____
10. _____
11. _____

Least Trusted   12. _____

Compare your rankings with those of your partner. Remember to use /ʌ/ each time you use the word *trust*. Did you agree about any professions?

_____

Did you have major disagreements about any professions?

_____

Check the answer key to see how your responses compare with Gallup's 2006 list.

Supplement 16: /ɜr/ *girl* – /ʌ/ *gull*

Fact 1. Students sometimes omit the /ɜr/ after mid-central vowels. They may say *gull* for *girl* or *hut* for *hurt*. Speakers of some dialects of North American English omit /ɜr/ after mid-central and other vowels and lengthen the vowels instead (e.g., hu:t, pa:k).

Fact 2. The /ɜr/ sound is usually spelled *-er* as in *her*, *-ir* as in *girl*, and *-ur* as in *fur*. Sometimes it is spelled *-or* as in *word, worry,* and *work.*

Fact 3. The /ɜr/ is a vowel and consonant sound blended together into one sound. For tips on placement for the /ɜr/, please see *Consonant Supplement 8*.

Listening Activity 1

CD 4; Track 54

Listen to /ɜr/: /ɜr/ . . . /ɜr/ . . . /ɜr/ . . . /ɜr/ . . . /ɜr/

Listening Activity 2

CD 4; Track 55

Listen to words with /ɜr/: *turn, shirt, word, heard, bird, girl, learn, work*

Listening Activity 3

CD 4; Track 56

Which word in each pair has the /ɜr/ sound – the first or the second? Close your book and write one or two on a piece of paper.

1. bun	burn		**4.** gull	girl	
2. turn	ton		**5.** hurt	hut	
3. shirt	shut		**6.** bud	bird	

Exercise 1

CD 4; Track 57

Repeat these words with /ɜr/.

tu**r**n	lea**r**n
shi**r**t	w**or**se
w**or**d	nu**r**se
hea**r**d	wo**r**k
bi**r**d	gi**r**l
w**e**re	thi**r**sty
fi**r**st	ce**r**tain

Exercise 2

CD 4; Track 58

Repeat the word pairs in Listening Activity 3.

Exercise 3

CD 4; Track 59

Practice the words with boldfaced letters silently.
Repeat the sentences. Look up from your book as you say each sentence.

1. I usually walk to w**or**k.

2. He has to leave w**or**k **ear**ly on Th**ur**sday.

3. My back h**ur**ts and it's getting w**or**se.

4. I h**ear**d the g**ir**l who lives next door is from G**er**many.

5. Are these sh**ir**ts d**ir**ty?

Exercise 4

Choose three words with /ɜr/ that are difficult or that you use frequently. Write a typical sentence you might say with each word. Practice the sentences.

a. _____

b. _____

c. _____

Supplement 17: /oʷ/ *note* – /ɑ/ *not*

Fact 1. The /oʷ/ glides upward. The /ɑ/ does not glide to another sound; it is a pure vowel sound.

Fact 2. Students sometimes confuse /ɑ/ for /oʷ/ so that *robe* sounds like *rob* and *hope* sounds like *hop*.

Listening Activity 1

CD 4; Track 60

Listen to the /oʷ/ sound: /oʷ/ . . . /oʷ/ . . . /oʷ/. . . /oʷ/

Listen to /oʷ/contrasted with /ɑ/: /oʷ/ . . . /ɑ/ . . . /oʷ/ . . . /ɑ/ . . . /oʷ/ . . . /ɑ/ . . . /oʷ/ . . . /ɑ/

Listening Activity 2

CD 4; Track 61

Listen to words with /oʷ/: *no, grow, soap, coast, vote, bone, loan, role, code, goal, promote, approach, appropriate, locate*

Listening Activity 3

Does the first or second word in each pair have the /oʷ/ sound? Close your book and write one or two on a separate piece of paper.

a. not	note	**e.** rod	road
b. cot	coat	**f.** soak	sock
c. coast	cost	**g.** rob	robe
d. cope	cop	**h.** wrote	rot

Check the answer key.

Listening Activity 4

Listen to your teacher, the speaker on audio, or your partner say one of the prompts in each pair. Give the correct response.

PROMPTS (STUDENT 1)	RESPONSES (STUDENT 2)
a. He has a scar.	(From the accident.)
He has a score.	(From the game.)
b. Tell John it's snowing.	(He'll be excited.)
Tell Joan it's snowing.	(She'll be excited.)
c. Did you take care of the knots?	(Yes. I untied them.)
Did you take care of the notes?	(Yes. I mailed them.)
d. Did you get the cod?	(No. The fish market was closed.)
Did you get the code?	(No. The programmer still has it.)

Check the answer key. Or check the answers with your partner.

Listening Activity 5

CD 4; Track 64

Listen to the paragraph. Fill in the blanks with words that have the /oʷ/ sound in stressed words and syllables. Check the answer key.

JOBS AND HORMONES

Testosterone, the hormone responsible for sex drive and aggression, may be a _____ in our choice of jobs. According to a study by a Georgia State University psychology professor, people with high levels of testosterone choose _____ in which they face severe competition to succeed. Actors have the _____ testosterone of all; doctors and trial lawyers rank high too. The _____ levels of testosterone are found among nurses and ministers, professionals who _____ themselves to comforting, not competing, with others. Because women have _____ levels of testosterone than men in general, the researcher cautions that success does not depend on hormones. Biology is important, but it is not destiny.

Exercise 1

CD 4; Track 65

Repeat the words with /oʷ/.

own	h**o**pe	l**o**w
over	cl**o**se	thr**ow**
open	h**o**me	kn**ow**
ozone	m**o**st	gr**ow**
odor	ph**o**ne	ag**o**
	d**o**n't	
	w**o**n't	
	al**o**ne	
	n**o**body	

Exercise 2

CD 4; Track 66

Repeat the word pairs in Listening Activity 3.

Exercise 3

Choose three words with /oʷ/ that you use frequently. Write typical sentences you might say with the words. Practice each sentence three times.

a. _____

b. _____

c. _____

Exercise 4

Practice the words with boldfaced letters silently.
Repeat the sentences. Look up from your book as you say each sentence.

CD 4; Track 67

a. She w**o**n't kn**ow** anyone there.

b. M**o**st of the time, I walk h**o**me.

c. I took careful n**o**tes.

d. He just wanted to be al**o**ne.

e. We've been trying to pr**o**mote recycling.

f. N**o**body's in the office next door.

g. I think they're ready to neg**o**tiate.

h. I h**o**pe you didn't thr**o**w it away.

Exercise 5

Record yourself reading *Jobs and Hormones* in Listening Activity 5 in the answer key. Monitor your pronunciation of the underlined words with /oʷ/. Summarize the paragraph in your own words.

Communicative Practice

What is important in a job? What motivates employees? Rate the following criteria contributing to job satisfaction. Then select the *three most important factors* and the *three least important factors*. First, preview words with /oʷ/: *most, proMOtion, low, own, aLONE, grow, MOtivate.*

Factors Contributing to Job Satisfaction

How important are these factors?

	Very Important	Important	Slightly Important	Not at All
Good Salary				
Job Security				
Health Benefits				
Flexible Hours				
Opportunity to Grow or Advance				
Participation in Decision-Making				
On-Site Day Care				
Being Your Own Boss				
Prestige				
Physical Activity				
Working Alone				
Working with People				
Working with Your Mind				
Chance to Be Creative				
Length of Commute				

Most Important Factors:

1. _____

2. _____

3. _____

Least Important Factors:

1. _____

2. _____

3. _____

In small groups, compare your answers. Did you agree? Did you rank the items from the perspective of an employee or a boss?

Info Gap Activities

Chapter 3, Exercise 3

Pages 24–25

Student A

CROSSWORD PUZZLE: Add the ending to each word and say the new word to your partner.

Number one has been done for you.

1. race + ial = **ra<u>ci</u>al**

2.

3. promote + ion =

4.

5. music + ian =

6.

7. precise + ion =

8.

9. divide + ion =

10.

Chapter 3, Exercise 3

Pages 24–25

Student B

CROSSWORD PUZZLE: Add the ending to each word and say the new word to your partner.

Number 2 has been done for you.

1.

2. create + ure = **crea<u>ture</u>**

3.

4. press + ure =

5.

6. event + ual =

7.

8. revise + ion =

9.

10. fuse + ion =

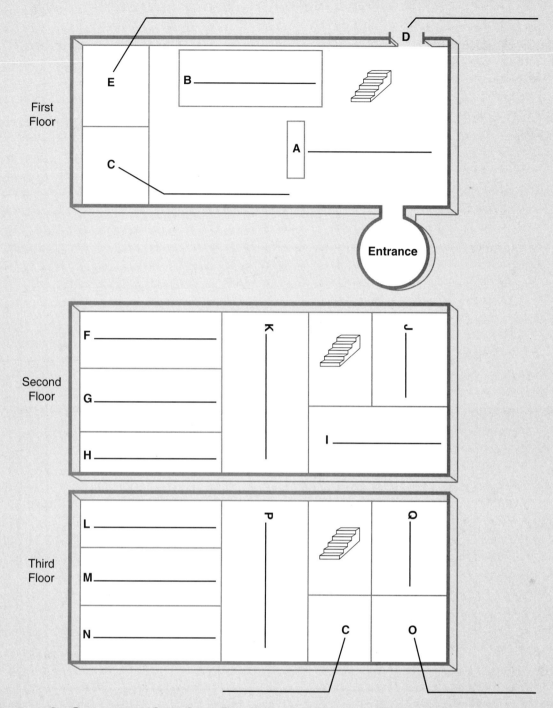

First
Floor

Entrance

Second
Floor

Third
Floor

Chapter 6, Communicative Practice: Library Orientation

Page 77

Student A

Check eight to ten areas of greatest interest:

☐ Rest Rooms
☐ Workstations/Databases
☐ Mathematics
☐ Education
☐ Photography Gallery
☐ Psychology
☐ Fire Exit

☐ Current periodicals/
　Foreign language
　newspapers
☐ Engineering
☐ Media/CDs/DVDs
☐ Cookbooks

☐ Circulation (checkout)
☐ Political Science
☐ Biological Sciences
☐ Anthropology
☐ Economics
☐ Copy Services

LIST OF COMMITMENTS

staff meeting	workshop	conference call
out-of-town	lunch meeting	car in shop
conference	language class	interview

SCHEDULE/ROLE B

Time	Monday	Tuesday	Wednesday	Thursday	Friday
9:00				English Pronunciation Class	
10:00					
11:00					
12:00					
1:00	Seminar				
2:00			Dentist		
3:00					
4:00					

Chapter 8, Communicative Practice: Announcing Schedule Changes

Page 120

> **Student A:** You might begin by saying, "Good morning. Before we get started today, I want to announce a few last minute schedule changes. First of all . . . "

WELCOME TO INTERNATIONAL STUDENT ORIENTATION
August 19

Dean's Welcome   Candler Chapel

9:00–~~9:30~~
  9:20

Immigration Sessions Student Center, Room ~~413~~, F-1 Visa Holders
          313

9:30–10:30   Student Center, Room 355, J-1 Visa Holders

Refreshment Break, Commons
10:30–10:45

Health Care in the U.S. Student Center Cinema

10:45–~~11:45~~   Student health insurance and the health care system
  11:55

Luncheon, 12:00–1:00, Student Center Ballroom

Campus Tours   Tour leaders leave from the lobby of the ~~Student Center~~. *Library*

~~1:00~~–2:30   The last tour departs at 2:00.
1:15

Transportation   Student Center ~~Ballroom~~ *Cinema*

3:00–4:00   City and campus transportation systems and costs

Chapter 10, Communicative Practice: Driving Test

Page 148

Student B: Mark questions 7 through 12 for thought groups. You can also mark the questions for the kinds of linking you just previewed. The first question has been marked.

DRIVING TEST

7. If you get‿sleepy while driving, / what should‿you do?

8. If you see a flashing red light at an intersection, what should you do?

9. If you see a flashing yellow light at an intersection, what should you do?

10. If your car's brakes fail, what should you do?

11. What's the minimum speed limit on the freeways in your state?

12. If you see trouble ahead, how should you warn the driver behind you?

Strategies for Independent Learning*

In this class, most of you have become aware of how to speak more clearly. Some of you have begun to make changes in your pronunciation, both conscious and unconscious, when speaking in class. Others have begun to make changes in pronunciation outside of class.

Unlearning old ways of speaking and learning new ways of speaking require continued practice. Here are some suggestions to help you 1) retain the progress you have made, and 2) continue to make long-term progress on your own. Some of these suggestions are new; others are a review of Helpful Hints from the text. Do not try to do everything. Choose the strategies that work best for *you*.

Suggestion 1

✔ **Take the time** and **make the conscious effort** to change. It won't happen automatically.

WHAT YOU CAN DO

1. Look at the Pronunciation Proficiency Scale in Chapter 1. Where were you at the beginning of the course? Where are you now? Where do you want to be in six months?

2. Look at the practice priorities in your "Speech Profile Form" in Chapter 1 and in your "Midcourse Self-Evaluation" at the end of Chapter 6. Write your current practice priorities below. Review them monthly.

a. _____

b. _____

c. _____

Suggestion 2

✔ **Overcome** any **resistance** you have to sounding like a speaker of English. Such resistance might be an **obstacle to progress.**

Changing pronunciation patterns involves changes in breathing, facial expression, and sometimes even body movement. You may feel less like a speaker of your native language. Be assured that you won't lose your accent completely. You will probably always sound like a speaker of your native language.

*Many of the principles and practice strategies in Appendix A are based on the ideas and insights of Joan Morley and William Acton. See the *Instructor's Manual* for a list of references.

1. Choose an English speaker you admire. Make this person your speaking model. Try to imitate everything about the way the speaker speaks and moves — gestures, facial expressions, and pronunciation.

2. Imagine your use of English speech patterns to be like a coat you can put on and take off as the situation requires.

3. Remember that your most important goals are to address patterns that interfere with understanding and that are highly distracting to the listener.

4. When you practice, imagine that you are an actor getting ready to go on the stage and that it is important for your audience to be able to hear and understand you.

Suggestion 3

✔ **Practice regularly** to achieve **long-term changes** in your pronunciation.

WHAT YOU CAN DO

1. **Schedule a regular** practice session each day. Ten minutes most days is ideal. Focus on your practice priorities:
   - Practice a new sound or stress pattern in words and phrases silently or in slow motion. Focus on how the pattern feels.
   - Practice a new sound or stress pattern out loud but with your eyes closed. Focus on how the pattern sounds.
   - Practice a new sound or stress pattern in sentences. Read the sentence (or thought group) and then look up and say it.
   - Mark a reading in a textbook, newspaper, etc., for thought groups or for occurrences of the particular sound, stress, or rhythm pattern you want to concentrate on. Record the reading, listen to it, and evaluate it for one pronunciation point.
   - Anticipate and silently rehearse what you think you will say in a class, a meeting, a discussion, a phone conversation, or an oral presentation. Record it and listen to it. Monitor your pronunciation of key words related to the topic.
   - Practice in front of a mirror. Mimic the mouth and facial movements of proficient speakers of English.
   - Record yourself reading a passage of at least 300 words from your field of work or study. Listen to the recording and take notes as if in a lecture. Write the important content words and omit the less important function words. Listen again and evaluate your use of overall rhythm patterns. Did you stress the content words and reduce the function words?

Recording Suggestions

You can use a computer to record yourself if you have the following: Windows® operating system, sound card, microphone, and speakers.

Click on Start —>All Programs —> Accessories —> Entertainment —> Sound Recorder

To record, click the red button.
To listen, click the Play button.
To increase volume, click on Effects.
To save, click on File —> Save as.

The Sound Recorder has a timer that records the length of your response.

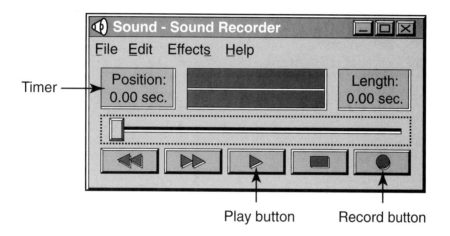

Timer

Play button   Record button

2. Self-monitor your speech in real-time for a short period — one minute — each day. Because it takes concentrated effort to be conscious of *what* you are saying and *how* you are saying it, don't try to self-monitor much longer than a minute or two each day. Choose a relaxed situation in which you have some control over the conversation.

3. Do not be anxious about errors. If you hear one, note it and go on. If it is convenient to self-correct, do so. You have to make errors in order to move forward.

4. Use a technique called tracking. In tracking, repeat what a proficient speaker of English is saying on a word-for-word basis, following about one or two words behind the speaker. At first, follow the intonation, speed, stress, and rhythm patterns by humming. As you become better at tracking, add words. You can track speakers on radio and television, as well as in real situations. You can track silently or out loud.

5. Seek the support of proficient English speakers. Tell trusted friends and coworkers that you have taken a course to improve your pronunciation. Tell them how they can assist you. Tell them you want to know if they don't understand you and if you want to be corrected.

6. Help speakers of English be good informants and models. If you ask English speakers how to pronounce words, their models may be exaggerated and unnatural. Ask the informants to say words in sentences, and you will probably hear more natural pronunciations.

7. Keep an oral diary or journal. Record thoughts and events of the day. Evaluate the recording by focusing on one pronunciation feature at a time. Listen for clear, as well as unclear, productions of specific pronunciation points.

8. Keep a list of words you encounter frequently and want to say clearly. Consult your dictionary for pronunciations. Practice the words often by saying them out loud once, then twice in a row, then three times in a row, and so on. Create typical sentences for the words or ask an English speaker to record the words in sentences for you so that you can practice by imitating the model or by speaking along with the model.

9. Keep a diary or log of unsuccessful interactions. Figure out what contributed to the communication breakdown. Remember that not all breakdowns are your fault. Communication is a two-way street.

10. Listen to short (15–20 second) segments of authentic speech. Transcribe it. You will need to listen over and over. If you have a written transcript, compare your written version with it — but not until you have picked up everything you can through listening on your own. Try this site: http://literacyworks. org/learningresources. It has audio and video broadcasts with transcripts.

11. Pay attention to what your listener needs to understand you. Different people and different kinds of speakers might need different modifications from you. Think of what you are working toward as accent addition, not reduction.

Suggestion 4

✔ **Practice with this text** (or parts of it) and the audio program **again and again.** A concept you may have missed the first time may become clear the second time. A skill that is in its early stages will become stronger with more practice.

Noun-Verb Pairs

Two-Syllable Noun-Verb Pairs with Stress Shift

Noun	Verb
1. ABstract	abSTRACT
2. ADdict	(to be) adDICT(ed)
3. CONduct	conDUCT
4. CONflict	conFLICT
5. CONstruct	conSTRUCT
6. CONtract	conTRACT
7. CONvert	conVERT
8. CONvict	conVICT
9. COMbat	comBAT
10. COMmune	comMUNE
11. DEfect	deFECT
12. DEsert	deSERT
13. DIScharge	disCHARGE
14. EScort	esCORT
15. EXploit	exPLOIT
16. EXtract	exTRACT
17. INcrease	inCREASE
18. INsert	inSERT
19. INsult	inSULT
20. IMplant	imPLANT
21. OBject	obJECT
22. PROtest	proTEST
23. PROgress	proGRESS
24. PERmit	perMIT
25. PREsent	preSENT
26. PROduce	proDUCE

Noun	Verb
27. PROject	proJECT
28. REbel	reBEL
29. REcord	reCORD
30. REcall	reCALL
31. REfuse	reFUSE
32. REject	reJECT
33. REprint	rePRINT
34. REwrite	reWRITE
35. SUBject	subJECT
36. SUSpect	susPECT
37. UPdate	upDATE

Two-Syllable Noun-Verb Pairs without Stress Shift

Noun	Verb
1. ANswer	ANswer
2. conCERN	conCERN
3. deBATE	deBATE
4. deLAY	deLAY
5. deSIGN	deSIGN
6. misTAKE	misTAKE
7. OFfer	OFfer
8. PROfit	PROfit
9. PROgram	PROgram
10. PROmise	PROmise
11. rePLY	rePLY
12. rePORT	rePORT
13. surPRISE	surPRISE

Guidelines for Word Stress

Most content words in conversational English (about 70 percent to 75 percent) are one-syllable and stressed on their only syllable. Stress in multi-syllable words varies. Although it is best to learn the stress pattern of each word, these *rules of thumb* will help you predict primary stress.

Do not memorize these guidelines. Instead, become aware of these regularities, and you will begin to notice patterns in the speech around you.

A. Regularities Based on Parts of Speech

1. Two-syllable nouns: Almost 90 percent have first-syllable stress.

Examples: FACtor, INput, CONcept

2. Two-syllable verbs: About 60 percent have second-syllable stress. About 75 percent of the two-syllable verbs in Coxhead's Academic Word List have second-syllable stress. (See Coxhead, A. 2000. A new academic word list. *TESOL Quarterly, 34[2]*, 213–8.)

Examples: beGIN, reCEIVE, conTAIN

See Appendix B for a list of two-syllable noun-verb pairs.

Examples: REject (noun) and reJECT (verb)

OBject (noun) and obJECT (verb)

3. Two-syllable verbs with prefixes (e.g., re-, de-, pre-): The stress is usually on the base or last element.

Examples: rePEAT, dePEND, preTEND

Stress patterns in verbs and nouns with longer prefixes.

Examples:

Verbs	Nouns
interFERE	INtercom
overPRICE	OVerpass
underSTAND	UNdershirt

4. Compound nouns and two-noun compounds: Most have primary stress on the first noun.

Examples: HEADache, BRIEFcase, WORD processor

Sometimes the first word in a compound is *not* a noun, but it is combined with a noun and considered to be a compound-like unit.

Examples: GREEN card, HOT dog, HIGH school

When the first noun is an ingredient in or component of the second noun, generally both nouns are stressed.

Examples: CREAM CHEESE, SILK TIE, COTton SHIRT, HAM SANDwich

5. Two-word verbs or verbs + particles: They are generally stressed more strongly on the particle.

Examples: to trade IN   She traded it IN.

to stop BY   Why don't you stop BY around eight?

Compare the stress patterns in the verb and noun forms:

Verbs	**Nouns**
We stop OVer in Singapore.	We have a brief STOPover.
When is the plane supposed to take OFF?	It was a smooth TAKEoff.

Note: The stress pattern of two-word verbs changes with a noun direct object:
She traded it IN.

She TRAded her CAR in.

She TRAded in her CAR.

6. Reflexive pronouns: Stress the last element.

Examples: mySELF, themSELVES

7. Compound adverbs: Usually stress the second element.

Examples: outSIDE, downTOWN, upSTAIRS, northEAST

8. Two-word proper names indicating place: Put stress on both elements but slightly more on the second word.*

Examples: MILLS COLlege, ELM AVenue, BURton ROAD, AMazon RIver, MOUNT EVerest, BLACK SEA, SUez caNAL, CAMbridge uniVERsity

*Note this exception: Street names with the word *street* generally have strong stress on the first element: MAIN Street, PEACHtree Street.

B. Regularities Based on Suffixes

Most words in English (about 70 percent) take suffixes that do not shift stress. They keep the same stress when suffixes are added.

> se LECT
>
> se LEC ting
>
> se LEC tion
>
> se LEC tive
>
> se LEC tor

1. Some of the more common suffixes that **do not** cause stress shift include the following.

-cy	SEcret	→	SEcrecy
-er	OFfice	→	OFficer
-ess	HOST	→	HOStess
-ful	MEAning	→	MEAningful
-ish	CHILD	→	CHILDish
-ism	BUDdha	→	BUDdhism
-ist	STRAtegy	→	STRAtegist
-less	HUmor	→	HUmorless
-like	LIFE	→	LIFElike
-ly	CAREful	→	CAREfully
-ment	inVEST	→	inVESTment
-ness	WILling	→	WILlingness
-or	coORdinate	→	coORdinator
-y	WIND	→	WINdy

2. Some of the more common suffixes that **do** cause stress shifts include the following. These first four suffixes account for almost 90 percent of all stress shifts. The stress shifts to **the syllable before these suffixes**:

-tion	LOcate	→	loCAtion
-ity	PERsonal	→	persoNALity
-ic	ALlergy	→	alLERGic
(-ic)al	HIStory	→	hisTORical

These suffixes are stressed:

-ee	NOminate	→	nomiNEE
-eer	ENgine	→	engiNEER
-ese	CHIna	→	ChiNESE
-ette	ciGAR	→	cigarETTE
-esque	STAtue	→	statuESQUE
-ique	TECHnical	→	techNIQUE

The stress shifts to **the syllable before these suffixes:**

-ial	MEmory	→	meMORial
	BEnefit	→	beneFIcial
	ESsence	→	esSENtial
-ian	CAnada	→	CaNAdian
	MUsic	→	muSIcian
	NORway	→	NorWEgian
-ient	sufFICE	→	sufFIcient
	nuTRItious	→	NUtrient
-ious	INdustry	→	inDUStrious
	SUSpect	→	susPIcious
-eous	COURage	→	couRAgeous
-uous	ambiGUity	→	amBIguous
-ify	SYLlable	→	sylLAbify
-cracy	DEmocrat	→	deMOcracy
-graphy	PHOtograph	→	phoTOgraphy
-logy	SOcial	→	sociOlogy

The stress falls **two syllables before this suffix:**

| -ate | | | CALculate |

Guidelines for Focus Words

Every thought group or short sentence has a focus word — a key word that gets more emphasis than the other words in the thought group. The focus word is generally longer in duration and has a major pitch change.

Basic or Neutral Focus

Why do we call attention to a certain word and not others? That depends on the situation and what is in the mind of the speaker, but here are some general guidelines summarized from Chapter 8.

Guideline 1: Focus is usually the last content word of a thought group or short sentence.

Example: Sue didn't **TELL** me about it.

Guideline 2: If the focus word is a compound or multi-syllable word, the primary stress of the focus word gets the pitch change.

Example: We haven't received our u**TIL**ity bill. (*utility bill* is a two-noun compound)

Guideline 3: Words and syllables in the thought group after the focus are backgrounded – there are no more major pitch changes after the focus.

Example: Alexis gave her **PHONE** number to me, / but I **LOST** it.

Special or Marked Focus

The focus can shift to a word other than the last content word in the thought group for several reasons.

Guideline 4: Focus highlights words that contrast with each other.

Example: Judy can **READ** Spanish / better than she can **SPEAK** it.

Sometimes the contrasting word or focus word is a function word that normally we do not stress.

Example: I put the sign-up sheet **NEXT** to the door, / not **ON** the door.

Guideline 5: Focus highlights new information.

Example: My major's **NUR**sing . . .

  pedi**A**tric nursing.

Guideline 6: Focus corrects or modifies a previous statement.

Example: X: We're having bean bur**RI**tos.

  Y: I thought we were having **BEEF** burritos.

Guideline 7: Focus emphasizes agreement.

Example: X: That was a great meal.

  Y: That **WAS** a great meal.

Guideline 8: Focus is used for general emphasis.

Example: The baby's **VER**y hungry.

Answer Key for : Selected Exercises

Chapter 8

Exercise 3, page 108

How would *you* divide the lecture segment below? Put a slash / at the end of each thought group. (*Note:* Optional thought groups are in parentheses.)

"Let's continue our discussion of pollution / Yesterday / we defined pollution / Today / we'll talk about the impact of pollution / its far-reaching effects / Many people think pollution (/) is just a problem for scientists / but it's not just a problem for scientists / It affects everyone / Because it affects human lives / it's a health problem / Because it affects property / it's an economic problem / And because it affects our appreciation of nature / it's an aesthetic problem"

Chapter 10

Exercise 5, page 147

Dictation. The teacher or the speaker on audio will say each sentence two times. Write each sentence.

How it sounds in casual speech: (What the teacher/speaker says.)	How it looks in written English: (What the students write.)
1. Cou-joo jus-thing-kabou-dit.	Could you just think about it?
2. Di-joo let-əm go?	Did you let them (or him) go?
3. They always cal-joo at work.	They always called you at work.
4. Can-choo fine-jer book?	Can't you find your book?
5. We look-cher number up.	We looked your number up.

Answer Key for Consonant Supplements

Supplement 2: Voiceless and Voiced Sounds

Exercise 2

1. ri**p** — (rib)
2. (code) — coat
3. (save) — safe
4. (age) — H
5. face — (phase)
6. (blog) — blo**ck**
7. proof — (prove)
8. half — (have)
9. wrote — (rode)
10. great — (grade)
11. (caused) — cost
12. ri**ch** — (ridge)

Exercise 3

1. view — (few)
2. (face) — vase
3. bush — (push)
4. (park) — bark
5. Greg — (Craig)
6. (cold) — gold
7. drip — (trip)
8. (town) — down
9. (cheap) — Jeep
10. (chain) — Jane

Supplement 5: /θ/ *thin*

Listening Activity 2

a. 1   **d.** 1   **g.** 2   **i.** 2

b. 1   **e.** 2   **h.** 1   **j.** 1

c. 2   **f.** 1

Listening Activity 3

a. It's not thick.

b. She wants to play baseball.

c. That's frightening.

d. I'm certain she's two now.

e. He can't solve the problem alone.

WHAT MAKES YOU THIN?

What makes you <u>thin</u>? Most people <u>think</u> that dieting is the answer, but researchers say that exercise is the best way to be thin. In one study, <u>thirty-two</u> men who were sedentary were put on an exercise program. They walked, jogged, and ran <u>throughout</u> the one-year program. The first <u>thing</u> the study showed was that the men who had exercised the most lost the most weight. The second <u>thing</u> the study revealed was that the men who lost the most weight ate more too. The researchers <u>theorize</u> that fat people don't really eat a lot. Their problem is that they are inactive.

Supplement 6: /f/ *fair*

Listening Activity 2

a. 1	**d.** 2	**g.** 1	**j.** 2
b. 1	**e.** 1	**h.** 2	**k.** 1
c. 2	**f.** 1	**i.** 1	**l.** 1

Listening Activity 3

a. That's why the coffee's so good.
b. Do you have proof?
c. We never get raises.
d. Did you see her go by?
e. In the houseware department.

Listening Activity 4

NEW WORDS AND PHRASES

Each year the American Dialect Society chooses one new word or <u>phrase</u> of the year. The members usually choose words that <u>reflect</u> the past year. They <u>favor</u> phrases that relate to current events. For example, in 199<u>5</u>, the phrase of the year was *World Wide Web*. In 1998, the new word was the <u>prefix</u> e- for *electronic*, as in *e-mail*. In 2006, the word of the year was *plutoed,* a term resulting from the <u>fact</u> that Pluto no longer fit the new way planets are <u>defined</u>.

Supplement 7: /ʃ/ *sheet*

Listening Activity 2

a. 1	**c.** 2	**e.** 2	**g.** 1	**i.** 2
b. 1	**d.** 1	**f.** 2	**h.** 2	**j.** 2

Listening Activity 3

a. His sheets.

b. Should I put it in the refrigerator?

c. Sure. I used to play baseball.

d. Although she wasn't responsible.

Listening Activity 4

SHYNESS

About 92 million Americans are <u>shy</u>. Researchers are taking an interest in shyness and have reached different conclusions. According to one study, <u>social</u> relations nowadays are more complex, and shyness is becoming a <u>national</u> concern. Another study found that only about half of the shy people were tense in <u>social</u> situations, contrary to popular belief. And still another study found that shy people tend to be more stable in their <u>relationships</u>. Some psychologists think that shyness may be inherited, whereas others think that shyness is cultural.

Supplement 8: /r/ *right*

Listening Activity 2

a. 2	**f.** 1	**k.** 2
b. 1	**g.** 2	**l.** 1
c. 2	**h.** 2	**m.** 1
d. 1	**i.** 1	**n.** 1
e. 1	**j.** 2	**o.** 2

Listening Activity 3

a. You need the short one.

b. At the mosque.

c. In the sky.

d. In first grade.

e. Not undergrad.

f. Oh, you must mean frat guys.

Listening Activity 4

BUTTERFLIES IN YOUR STOMACH

If you've ever given a <u>report</u> in front of a class or a group of people, you know the feeling. Your heart <u>races</u>, your blood pressure <u>rises</u>, your hands start to shake, your throat gets <u>dry</u>, and you get butterflies in your stomach. What causes your body to <u>react</u> this way? When you're nervous, your glands <u>release</u> adrenaline into your bloodstream. The adrenaline causes your muscles to tense up. It also causes increased motion in your stomach muscles. As a <u>result</u>, your stomach <u>produces</u> more acid than it needs for digestion. The acid feels like butterflies in your stomach.

Supplement 9: /v/ *very*

Listening Activity 2

a. 1	**e.** 2	**h.** 1	**k.** 2
b. 1	**f.** 1	**i.** 1	**l.** 1
c. 2	**g.** 1	**j.** 2	**m.** 1
d. 1			

Listening Activity 3

a. On the bike.

b. One with blue flowers.

c. They remind me of her.

d. The engine died.

e. The cows?

Listening Activity 4

VALENTINE'S DAY

All <u>over</u> the world, it is popular to <u>give</u> cards, flowers, gifts, and other tokens of <u>love</u> on February 14, St. Valentine's Day. There are <u>several</u> explanations for the origin of this holiday; <u>however</u>, the most believable is that St. Valentine's Day is a <u>survival</u> of a February 15th Roman <u>festival</u>. During this festival, bachelors picked names of women to <u>discover</u> who their "valentines" would be for the coming year. The couples then exchanged gifts and sometimes even became engaged.

Answer Key for Vowel Supplements

Supplement 10

Exercise 1

1. spread
rounded

2. high
low

Supplement 13: /ɪ/ *fit*

Listening Activity 3

a. 1	**c.** 2	**e.** 2	**g.** 2	**i.** 1
b. 1	**d.** 2	**f.** 1	**h.** 1	**j.** 2

Listening Activity 4

a. Yeah! On that ice.

b. It was a good crop.

c. Yes. She's packing her bags.

d. Yes, with the hammer.

e. In the medicine cabinet.

Listening Activity 5

DRINKING AND HEALTH RISKS

People often <u>lift</u> a glass to toast good health. Drinking may indeed lower the <u>risk</u> of several diseases, according to <u>statistics</u> released by the Harvard School of Public Health. Researchers found that one to two <u>drinks</u> each day reduced the risk of heart disease by about twenty-<u>six</u> percent in men and up to <u>fifty</u> percent in women. Researchers warn, however, that drinking can increase other health risks. Alcohol is <u>linked</u> to a higher risk of breast cancer in women and to a higher rate of <u>liver</u> disease.

Supplement 14: /ɛ/ *pen*

Listening Activity 3

a. 2	**d.** 1	**g.** 1	**j.** 1
b. 2	**e.** 2	**h.** 2	**k.** 2
c. 1	**f.** 1	**i.** 1	**l.** 1

Listening Activity 4

a. For dinner.

b. Sorry you missed him.

c. Too spicy.

d. Did you like him?

e. Not too old and not too young.

Listening Activity 5

AIRBAGS

Airbags have become standard equipment in new cars. They are stored in the <u>center</u> of the steering wheel, in the instrument panel, in the doors, and sometimes in the roof. In an accident, they quickly inflate to <u>help</u> save lives. But how do they work? Airbags have electronic <u>sensors</u> that can feel a crash as it begins to happen. The sensors <u>set</u> off a gas that rushes into the bags. The soft bags <u>protect</u> the people in the car, and <u>then</u> the bags deflate.

Supplement 15: /ʌ/ *luck*

Listening Activity 3

a. 2	**c.** 1	**e.** 1	**g.** 1
b. 2	**d.** 1	**f.** 2	**h.** 1

Listening Activity 4

a. Yes. It has fur.

b. For coffee.

c. I hate that shade of green.

d. I can't untie it.

e. No. I lost.

NUMBERS OF FOREIGN-BORN ARE UP IN U.S.

Based on the results of a <u>study</u> in 2002, the Census Bureau reported that more than <u>one</u> in every 10 residents of the United States was foreign-born. The number was more than <u>double</u> the percentage of foreign born in 1970 (4.8%). <u>Much</u> of the foreign-born population—almost one third—resides in California. New York ranks second and Florida third. The government study also includes where immigrants are <u>from</u>. One of every two foreign-born residents <u>comes</u> from Central and South America and the Caribbean.

Communicative Practice

Most Trusted:
1. Nurses
2. Pharmacists
3. Veterinarians
4. Dentists
5. College teachers
6. Police officers
7. Bankers
8. State governors
9. Business executives
10. Lawyers
11. Senators
Least Trusted:
12. Insurance salespeople

Supplement 16: /ɜr/ *girl*

Listening Activity 3

1. 2   **4.** 2

2. 1   **5.** 1

3. 1   **6.** 2

Supplement 17: /oʷ/ *note*

Listening Activity 3

a. 2	**d.** 1	**g.** 2
b. 2	**e.** 2	**h.** 1
c. 1	**f.** 1	

Listening Activity 4

a. From the game.

b. He'll be excited.

c. Yes. I mailed them.

d. No. The fish market was closed.

Listening Activity 5

JOBS AND HORMONES

Testosterone, the hormone responsible for sex drive and aggression, may be a component in our choice of jobs. According to a study by a Georgia State University psychology professor, people with high levels of testosterone choose roles in which they face severe competition to succeed. Actors have the most testosterone of all; doctors and trial lawyers rank high, too. The lowest levels of testosterone are found among nurses and ministers, professionals who devote themselves to comforting, not competing with, others. Because women have lower levels of testosterone than men in general, the researcher cautions that success does not depend on hormones. Biology is important, but it is not destiny.

Index

/a/, 186, 187, /ʌ/ versus, 196–199

Abbreviations, stress in, 66

actually, introducing corrections
    with, 115

Addressing women, 32

Adjectives
    with *-ate,* 76
    stress on, 90

Adverbs
    with *-ate,* 76
    compound, stress in, 57
    stress on, 90

/æ/, 185,
    /ɛ/ versus, 193–196

Agreement, focus highlighting, 116

/aɪ/, 187

Air fares, checking, 153

Announcing schedule changes, 120

Appointments, scheduling,
    100–101

Articles, reducing or weakening,
    90, 96

-ate, stress and, 74–75, 76

/aʊ/, 187

/b/, 155, 159, 161
    as final sound, linking with word
        beginning with consonant,
        144
    as voiced consonant, 29–30, 156–158
    /v/ versus, 180–184

Background knowledge, rising
    intonation to check, 131

Beats (*see* Syllables)

Business practices, comparing, 122

can't/can, confusing, 98–99

-cc-, 26

Certainty, falling intonation
    expressing, 125–126

-ch-, 22, 23

Choices, intonation in questions and
    statements giving, 132

Chunks, 106 (see also Thought groups)

-ci-, 21

Clarification, rising intonation to
    request, 127–128

Color preference, 38

Comparing business practices, 122

Confirmation, rising intonation
    indicating desire for, 126

Conjunctions, reducing or weakening,
    90, 96

Connected speech (see Linking)

Connecting words, 46 (see also Linking)

Consonants, 19–36
    /b/, 29, 30, 144, 155, 156–158, 159,
        161, 180–184
    continuants and stops, 159–160
    /d/, 29, 30, 61, 144, 146, 147, 155,
        156–158, 159, 161
    /dʒ/, 19, 23, 147, 155, 156, 161
    /ð/, 155, 156, 161
    /ʒ/, 19, 23, 155, 156, 161
    /f/, 29, 31, 155, 156, 159, 161,
        162–165, 165–169
    final, 28–33, 157, 159–160, 161
    final clusters ending in /s/, 42–43
    /g/, 19, 29, 30, 144, 155, 156–158,
        159, 161
    /h/, 19, 155, 161
    /k/, 22, 25, 29–30, 144, 155,
        156–158, 159, 161
    /kw/, 25
    /l/, 155, 156, 161, 174–180
    linking (*see* Linking)
    /m/, 155, 156, 161
    /ŋ/, 155, 161
    /n/, 146, 155, 161
    /p/, 29, 30, 144, 155, 156–158, 159,
        161, 166–169
    phonetic alphabet, 155

/r/, 155, 161, 174–180
    tap or flap, 174
/s/, 29, 31, 39–44, 155, 156, 159, 161,
    162–165
/ʃ/, 19, 21, 22, 23, 155, 156, 161,
    170–173
speech pathway and consonant
    chart, 160–162
strategies for learning, 35
/t/, 29, 30, 61, 146, 147, 155,
    156–158, 159–161, 162–165
/ð/, 155, 156, 161
/θ/, 155, 156, 161, 162–165
/tʃ/, 22, 23, 147, 155, 156, 161,
    170–173
unusual spelling patterns, 21–28
/v/, 29, 31, 32, 155, 156, 161, 180–184
voiced and voiceless, 23, 28–33,
    156–158
/w/, 155, 161, 180–184
/y/, 147, 155, 161
/z/, 29, 31–32, 40, 43, 155, 156–157,
    161

Content words, stress on, 90–102

Continuants, 159–160

Contrast, focus highlighting, 110–112, 223

Corrections
    focus highlighting, 115–116, 224
    introducing with *actually,* 115

/d/, 45, 155, 161
    as final sound, 144, 146
    in numbers, 61
    as voiced consonant, 29–30, 156–158
    /y/ linked with, 147

/dʒ/, 19, 23, 147, 155, 156

Deletion, see Omission

Dictionary, 9–18
    consonant sounds in, 13, 16
    introduction to symbols in, 9
    schwa vowel sound in, 13, 17

stress in, 10–11

syllables in, 10

vowels with base sounds in, 12, 17

vowels with name sounds in, 11, 17

Discussion, 79–81

"Dream Deferred," (Hughes), 133

Driving test, 148

-du-, 23

/ʒ/, 19, 23, 155, 156, 161

/ɛ/, 185, 187

/eʸ/ and /æ/ versus, 193–196

-ed

stress and, 75

verbs ending with, 45–49

-ee, stress and, 73, 222

-eer, stress and, 73, 222

-ese, stress and, 73, 222

-esque, stress and, 73, 222

-ette, stress and, 73, 222

Evacuating your home, 33–34

/ɛ/, 185, 187

/eʸ/ versus, 185, 187, 193–196

/ɛ/ versus, 193–196

/f/, 155, 156, 159, 161

/p/ versus, 165–169

/θ/ versus, 162–165

as voiceless consonant, 29, 31

Fable, 48

False statements, 47

Focus words, 103, 108–121, 223–224

compound or multi-syllable words
as, 109–110

normal or basic focus, 108–109, 223

special or marked focus, 110–116,
223–224

Food orders, placing, 145

Function words, reducing or weakening,
90–102

/g/, 19, 23, 155, 159, 161

as final sound, linking with
word beginning with
consonant, 144

as voiced consonant, 29, 30, 156–158

Goal setting, 7–8, 213

Graphs, 50–53

-graphy, stress and, 73, 222

/h/, 19, 155, 161

-ial, stress and, 72, 222

-ian, stress and, 72, 222

-ic, stress and, 69, 72, 221

-ical, stress and, 72, 221

-ify, stress and, 72, 222

/ɪ/, 185, 187

/iʸ/ versus, 189–193

Interjections, stress on, 90

Interviews, 139

Intonation, 123–140

at end of non-final thought groups,
134–139

falling, at end of sentences, 123,
125–126, 128, 130

rising, at end of sentences, 123,
126–132

in series, 137

-ion, stress and, 69, 72, 75, 221

-ious, stress and, 72, 222

-ique, stress and, 73, 222

/ɜr/, 186, 187

/ʌ/ versus, 200–201

-ity, stress and, 69, 72, 221

/iy/, 185, 187

/ɪ/ versus, 189–193

/k/, 22, 25, 155, 159, 161

as final sound, linking with word
beginning with consonant,
144

as voiceless consonant, 29–30,
156–158

Knock! Knock! jokes, 102

/kw/, 25

/l/, 155, 156, 161

/r/ versus, 174–180

Library crad, applying for, 83

Library orientation, 77

Linking, 141–148

consonant to consonant, 143–148

consonant to vowel, 143

/d/ to /y/, 147

stop consonant to consonant,
144–145

/t/ to /y/, 147

Linking words, 46

Listen!, 20–21, 37–39, 55–56, 70–71,
86–89, 103–106, 138

-logy, stress and, 73, 222

/m/, 155, 156, 161

Midcourse self-evaluation, 84, 213

Modifications, focus highlighting,
115–116, 224

/ŋ/, 155, 156, 161

/n/, 146, 155, 156, 161

Needs and attitudes assessment, 5–7

Negatives, stress on, 90, 99

New information, focus highlighting,
112, 114, 224

No e-mail Fridays, 67–68

Nouns

ending in -ate, stress in 76

compound, stress in, 57–61, 220

stress on, 90

two-noun compounds, stress in, 60,
220

two-syllable, stress in, 57, 63, 219

two-syllable verbs also used as,
stress in, 63, 217–218

Numbers, stress in, 61–62

/oʷ/, 186, 187, 189

/aᵃ/ versus, 201–205

/ɔ/, 186, 187

/ɔɪ/, 187

/p/, 155, 159, 161

as final sound, linking with word
beginning with consonant, 144

/f/ versus, 165–169

as voiceless consonant, 29–30,
156–158

Omission, of –h, 90, 96–97, 143

Personal goals, setting, 7–8, 213

Pitch (see aslo Intonation), 55, 106–108

Prepositions, reducing or weakening,
90, 96

Presentation, process, 149–150

Pronouns
 reducing or weakening, 90, 96
 reflexive, stress in, 57, 220

Pronunciation guide, 16–17

Pronunciation proficiency scale, 8

Pronunciation profile, 1–8

Proverbs, 44

qu-, 25

-qu-, 25

Questions
 presenting choices, intonation in,
  132
 -wh questions, intonation at end of,
  130–131
 yes/no questions intonation at end
  of, 128–130

/r/, 155, 156, 161
 /l/ versus, 174–180

Rapport, rising intonation to establish,
 131–132

Reduced words, rhythm and, 85–102

Repetition, rising intonation to request,
 130–131

Resistance to pronunciation change,
 overcoming, 93, 213–214

Rhythm, 85–102

-s, 38–44, 50

/s/ 40, 155, 156, 161
 as voiceless consonant, 29–30,
  156–158
 words ending in two consonant
  sounds with, 42
 final, in words spelled the
  same and pronounced
  differently, 31

Schedule changes, announcing, 120

Scheduling an appointment, 100–101

Schwa (ə), 13, 17, 71, 95–96

Sentences, falling intonation at end
 indicating completion of idea, 125

Series, intonation in, 137

Setting personal goals, 7–8

sh-, 23

/ʃ/, 155, 156, 170–173
 spellings, 19, 21, 22, 23
 -si-, 23

Small-group discussion, 79–81

Speech pathway, 160–161

Speech profile, 1–5

Spelling
 consonants with unusual spelling
  patterns, 21–26

-ssi-, 21

-ssu-, 21

Statements
 presenting choices, intonation in, 132
 rising intonation at end to request
  clarification, 127

Stops, 159–160, 161
 linking, 144

Strategies for independent learning,
 213–216

Stress initial voicelss and voiced, 158
 word in dictionary, 10–11
 equal, on every word and
  syllable, 86
 in phrases and sentences
  (*see* Rhythm)
 in words, based on parts of speech,
  55–68, 219–220
 in words, based on suffixes or
  word endings, 69–83, 221–222
 on important content words, 90
 primary, 10–11, 55, 56, 57, 109
 secondary, 56, 75

-su-, 19, 23

Suffixes, predicting stress using, 69–76

Surprise, rising intonation indicating, 126

Surveys, 139

Syllables, 37
 in dictionary, 10
 with *-ed* endings, 45–46
 with *-s* endings, 39–41

/t/, 45, 146, 155, 159, 161
 linked with /y/, 147
 in -teen numbers, 61
 /θ/ versus, 162–165
 as voiceless consonant, 29–30,
  156–158

/ð/, 155, 156, 161

/θ/, 155, 156, 161
 /s/, /t/, and /f/ versus, 162–165

Thought groups, 103–104, 106–108
 non-final, intonation at end of,
  134–139

-ti-, 19, 21, 22

TOEFL® iBT Practices, 49, 74, 119,
 136–137

Tracking, 215

/tʃ/, 22, 23, 155, 156
 /ʃ/ versus, 170–173

-tu-, 22

/ʌ/, 186, 187
 /ɜr/ versus, 200–201
 /oʷ/ versus, 196–199

Uncertainty, rising intonation indicating,
 126

"Upspeak," 131

/uʷ/, 185, 186, 187

/v/, 155, 161
 as voiced consonant, 29, 156–157
 /w/ and /b/ versus, 180–184

Verbs
 auxiliary, reducing or weakening,
  90, 96
 with base and prefix, stress in,
  62, 219
 main, stress on, 90
 regular, with *-ed* endings, 45
 two-syllable, also used as nouns,
  stress in, 63, 217–218
 two-word, stress in, 64, 220

Voiced consonants, 23, 28–33, 156–158

Voiceless consonants, 23, 28–33, 156–158

Vowels
 /ə/, 13, 17, 71, 95–96, 186, 187
 /ɑ/, 186, 187, 188, 196–199, 201–205
 /æ/, 185, 187, 188
 /eʸ/, 185, 187, 188, 193–195
 /aɪ/, 187
 /aʊ/, 187
 back, 186
 base, 12
 central, 186

consonants linked to, 143

diphthongs, 186–187

/ɛ/, 185, 187, 188, 189, 193–196

/ɪ/, 185, 187, 188, 189–192

/iʸ/, 185, 187, 188, 189-192

front, 185

/ɝr/, 186, 200–201

lax, 188–189

name (long), 11

/ʊ/, 186, 187, 188, 189

/uʷ/, 185, 186, 187, 188, 189

/oʷ/, 186, 187, 188, 189, 201–205

phonetic alphabet and vowel chart,
187

/ɔ/, 186, 187

/ɔɪ/, 187

schwa, 13, 17, 71, 95–96

tense, 188–189

/ʌ/, 186, 196–199

/ə/, 13, 17, 71, 95-96

/w/, 155, 156, 161

/v/ versus, 180–184

wh- questions, intonation at end
of, 130

wh- words, stress on, 90

Women, addressing, 32

-x-, 26

/ʊ/, 186, 187, 188, 189

/uʷ/, 186, 187, 188

/y/, 155, 156, 161

/d/ linked with, 147

/t/ linked with, 147

yes/no questions, rising intonation at
end of, 128–129

/z/, 40, 155, 156, 161

as voiced consonant, 29–30,
156–158

words ending in two consonant
sounds with, 42

final, in words spelled the
same and pronounced
differently, 31

CD 1

Track	Chapter	Pages	Title
1	2	10	Exercise 1
2	2	11	Exercise 2
3	2	12	Exercise 3
4	2	12	Exercise 4
5	2	13	Exercise 5
6	2	13	Exercise 6
7	2	16–17	Pronunciation Guide for Well Said
8	3	20	Listening Activity 1
9	3	21	Listening Activity 2
10	3	21	Rule 3-1
11	3	22	Rule 3-2
12	3	22	Exercise 1
13	3	23	Rule 3-3
14	3	23	Rule 3-4
15	3	24	Exercise 2
16	3	25	Rule 3-5
17	3	26	Rule 3-6
18	3	26	Exercise 4
19	3	29	Rule 3-7
20	3	29	Rule 3-7: Complete the Rule
21	3	30	Exercise 6
22	3	31	Rule 3-8
23	3	31	Exercise 7
24	3	32	Exercise 8
25	3	33	Exercise 9
26	4	37	Syllables and Word Endings
27	4	37	Listening Activity 1
28	4	37	Listening Activity 1
29	4	38	Listening Activity 2
30	4	38	Listening Activity 2
31	4	39	Listening Activity 3
32	4	39	Rule 4-1
33	4	40	Exercise 1
34	4	41	Exercise 2
35	4	41	Exercise 3
36	4	42	Exercise 4
37	4	43	Exercise 5, Part A
38	4	43	Exercise 5, Part B
39	4	43	Exercise 6, Part A
40	4	43	Exercise 6, Part B
41	4	44	Exercise 7
42	4	45	Rule 4-2
43	4	45	Exercise 8
44	4	46	Exercise 9
45	4	47	Exercise 10

CD 2

Track	Chapter	Pages	Title
1	5	55	Listening Activity 1
2	5	55–56	Listening Activity 1
3	5	56	Listening Activity 2
4	5	57	Rule 5-1
5	5	57	Rule 5-2
6	5	57	Rule 5-3
7	5	58	Exercise 1
8	5	60	Rule 5-4
9	5	61	Rule 5-5
10	5	62	Exercise 5
11	5	62	Rule 5-6
12	5	63	Rule 5-7
13	5	63	Rule 5-7
14	5	63	Exercise 6
15	5	64	Rule 5-8
16	5	65	Exercise 8
17	5	66	Exercise 9
18	6	70	Listening Activity 1
19	6	70	Listening Activity 1
20	6	71	Listening Activity 2
21	6	71	Listening Activity 3
22	6	72	Rule 6-1
23	6	72–73	Exercise 1
24	6	73	Rule 6-2
25	6	73	Rule 6-3
26	6	74	Exercise 2
27	6	74	Rule 6-4
28	6	75	Exercise 3
29	6	76	Exercise 4
30	7	86	Listening Activity 1
31	7	86–87	Listening Activity 2
32	7	86–87	Listening Activity 2
33	7	87	Listening Activity 3
34	7	88	Listening Activity 4: Part A
35	7	88	Listening Activity 4: Part B
36	7	89	Listening Activity 4: Part C
37	7	91	Exercise 1
38	7	91–92	Exercise 2
39	7	92	Exercise 3
40	7	94	Exercise 4
41	7	94–95	Exercise 5
42	7	96–97	Exercise 6
43	7	97	Exercise 7
44	7	98	Exercise 8
45	7	99	Exercise 9
46	8	103	Listening Activity 1
47	8	104	Listening Activity 2: Part A
48	8	105	Listening Activity 2: Part B
49	8	105	Sentence 1
50	8	105	Sentence 2
51	8	105	Sentence 3
52	8	105	Sentence 4
53	8	105	Sentence 5
54	8	105	Sentence 6
55	8	105	Sentence 7
56	8	105	Sentence 8
57	8	105	Listening Activity 3
58	8	105–106	Listening Activity 3
59	8	106	Rule 8-1
60	8	107	Exercise 2
61	8	108	Exercise 3
62	8	108–109	Rule 8-2
63	8	109	Exercise 4
64	8	109	Rule 8-3
65	8	110	Exercise 5
66	8	110–111	Rule 8-4
67	8	111–112	Exercise 6

CD 3

Track	Chapter	Pages	Title
1	8	112	Rule 8-5
2	8	113–114	Exercise 7
3	8	114	Exercise 8
4	8	115	Rule 8-6
5	8	115–116	Exercise 9
6	8	116	Rule 8-7
7	8	117	Prime-Time Practice
8	8	117	Sentence 1
9	8	117	Sentence 2
10	8	117	Sentence 3
11	8	117	Sentence 4
12	8	117	Sentence 5
13	8	117	Sentence 6
14	8	117	Sentence 7
15	8	117	Sentence 8

Track	Chapter	Pages	Title
16	8	117	Sentence 9
17	8	117	Sentence 10
18	8	117	Sentence 11
19	8	118	Exercise 11
20	9	123–124	Listening Activity 1
21	9	124	Listening Activity 2
22	9	124–125	Listening Activity 3
23	9	125	Rule 9-1
24	9	126	Rule 9-2
25	9	126	Exercise 1: Part A
26	9	127	Exercise 1: Part B
27	9	127	Rule 9-3
28	9	128	Exercise 2
29	9	128	Rule 9-4
30	9	129	Exercise 3: Part A
31	9	130	Exercise 3: Part B
32	9	130	Rule 9-5
33	9	131	Rule 9-6
34	9	132	Exercise 5: Part A
35	9	132	Rule 9-7
36	9	132–133	Exercise 6
37	9	133	Prime-Time Practice
38	9	135	Exercise 7
39	9	135	Exercise 7
40	9	135	Rule 9-8
41	9	136	Exercise 8: Anecdote 1
42	9	136	Exercise 8: Anecdote 2
43	9	136–137	Exercise 9
44	9	137	Rule 9-9
45	10	142	Listening Activity
46	10	143	Rule 10-1
47	10	143	Rule 10-2
48	10	143	Exercise 1: Part A
49	10	144	Rule 10-3
50	10	144–145	Exercise 4
51	10	146	A Helpful Hint
52	10	146	Exercise 6
53	10	147	Rule 10-4
54	10	147	Rule 10-5
55	10	147	Exercise 7
56	Consonant Supplements	155	Supplement 1: Exercise 1
57	Consonant Supplements	156	Supplement 2: Exercise 1
58	Consonant Supplements	157	Supplement 2: Exercise 2
59	Consonant Supplements	157	Supplement 2: Exercise 2
60	Consonant Supplements	157	Supplement 2: Exercise 3
61	Consonant Supplements	158	Supplement 2: Exercise 4
62	Consonant Supplements	159	Supplement 3
63	Consonant Supplements	160	Supplement 3: Exercise 1
64	Consonant Supplements	162	Supplement 5: Listening Activity 1
65	Consonant Supplements	162	Supplement 5: Listening Activity 2
66	Consonant Supplements	162	Supplement 5: Listening Activity 3
67	Consonant Supplements	163	Supplement 5: Listening Activity 4
68	Consonant Supplements	164	Supplement 5: Exercise 1
69	Consonant Supplements	164	Supplement 5: Exercise 2
70	Consonant Supplements	164	Supplement 5: Exercise 4
71	Consonant Supplements	164	Supplement 5: Exercise 5
72	Consonant Supplements	166	Supplement 6: Listening Activity 1
73	Consonant Supplements	166	Supplement 6: Listening Activity 2
74	Consonant Supplements	166	Supplement 6: Listening Activity 3
75	Consonant Supplements	167	Supplement 6: Listening Activity 4
76	Consonant Supplements	168	Supplement 6: Exercise 1
77	Consonant Supplements	168	Supplement 6: Exercise 2
78	Consonant Supplements	168	Supplement 6: Exercise 4
79	Consonant Supplements	169	Supplement 6: Exercise 5

CD 4

Track	Chapter	Pages	Title
1	Consonant Supplements	170	Supplement 7: Listening Activity 1
2	Consonant Supplements	170	Supplement 7: Listening Activity 2
3	Consonant Supplements	170	Supplement 7: Listening Activity 3
4	Consonant Supplements	171	Supplement 7: Listening Activity 4
5	Consonant Supplements	172	Supplement 7: Exercise 1
6	Consonant Supplements	172	Supplement 7: Exercise 2
7	Consonant Supplements	172	Supplement 7: Exercise 4
8	Consonant Supplements	173	Supplement 7: Exercise 5
9	Consonant Supplements	174	Supplement 8: Listening Activity 1
10	Consonant Supplements	174	Supplement 8: Listening Activity 2
11	Consonant Supplements	175	Supplement 8: Listening Activity 3
12	Consonant Supplements	175	Supplement 8: Listening Activity 4
13	Consonant Supplements	177	Supplement 8: Exercise 1
14	Consonant Supplements	177	Supplement 8: Exercise 2
15	Consonant Supplements	177	Supplement 8: Exercise 4
16	Consonant Supplements	177	Supplement 8: Exercise 5
17	Consonant Supplements	180	Supplement 9: Listening Activity 1
18	Consonant Supplements	180	Supplement 9: Listening Activity 2
19	Consonant Supplements	180	Supplement 9: Listening Activity 3
20	Consonant Supplements	181	Supplement 9: Listening Activity 4
21	Consonant Supplements	182	Supplement 9: Exercise 1
22	Consonant Supplements	182	Supplement 9: Exercise 2

23	Consonant Supplements	183	Supplement 9: Exercise 4
24	Consonant Supplements	183	Supplement 9: Exercise 5
25	Vowel Supplements	185	Supplement 10: Exercise 2
26	Vowel Supplements	186	Supplement 10: Exercise 3
27	Vowel Supplements	186	Supplement 10: Exercise 4
28	Vowel Supplements	187	Supplement 10: Exercise 5
29	Vowel Supplements	188	Supplement 12: Exercise 1
30	Vowel Supplements	189	Supplement 13: Listening Activity 1
31	Vowel Supplements	189	Supplement 13: Listening Activity 2
32	Vowel Supplements	190	Supplement 13: Listening Activity 3
33	Vowel Supplements	190	Supplement 13: Listening Activity 4
34	Vowel Supplements	191	Supplement 13: Listening Activity 5
35	Vowel Supplements	191	Supplement 13: Exercise 1
36	Vowel Supplements	191	Supplement 13: Exercise 2
37	Vowel Supplements	192	Supplement 13: Exercise 4
38	Vowel Supplements	193	Supplement 14: Listening Activity 1
39	Vowel Supplements	193	Supplement 14: Listening Activity 2
40	Vowel Supplements	193	Supplement 14: Listening Activity 3
41	Vowel Supplements	194	Supplement 14: Listening Activity 4
42	Vowel Supplements	194	Supplement 14: Listening Activity 5
43	Vowel Supplements	195	Supplement 14: Exercise 1
44	Vowel Supplements	195	Supplement 14: Exercise 2
45	Vowel Supplements	195	Supplement 14: Exercise 4

46	Vowel Supplements	196	Supplement 15: Listening Activity 1
47	Vowel Supplements	196	Supplement 15: Listening Activity 2
48	Vowel Supplements	197	Supplement 15: Listening Activity 3
49	Vowel Supplements	197	Supplement 15: Listening Activity 4
50	Vowel Supplements	197	Supplement 15: Listening Activity 5
51	Vowel Supplements	198	Supplement 15: Exercise 1
52	Vowel Supplements	198	Supplement 15: Exercise 2
53	Vowel Supplements	198	Supplement 15: Exercise 4
54	Vowel Supplements	200	Supplement 16: Listening Activity 1
55	Vowel Supplements	200	Supplement 16: Listening Activity 2
56	Vowel Supplements	200	Supplement 16: Listening Activity 3
57	Vowel Supplements	200	Supplement 16: Exercise 1
58	Vowel Supplements	201	Supplement 16: Exercise 2
59	Vowel Supplements	201	Supplement 16: Exercise 3
60	Vowel Supplements	201	Supplement 17: Listening Activity 1
61	Vowel Supplements	201	Supplement 17: Listening Activity 2
62	Vowel Supplements	202	Supplement 17: Listening Activity 3
63	Vowel Supplements	202	Supplement 17: Listening Activity 4
64	Vowel Supplements	202	Supplement 17: Listening Activity 5
65	Vowel Supplements	203	Supplement 17: Exercise 1
66	Vowel Supplements	203	Supplement 17: Exercise 2
67	Vowel Supplements	203	Supplement 17: Exercise 4

Fria,
Como un vaso frio,
ese es tu vicio,
te caiste ~~en el~~ piso,
       al
te rompiste en mil
pedazos,
por la suerte has
fracasado en intentos,
con personas que no
valen la pena es
una perdida de
tiempo,
Yo admito que no sere
perfecta,
pero tu eres mi pasatiempo,
a una adicta,
a ese corazon herido,
que Yo solo ~~M~~ quiero sanar,
y ~~ademas~~ incondicional amar.
Eres mi nuevo vicio!

Eres Mi Nuevo Vicio

tomame o dejame
Pero no me pidas

and
either or
not only but also
Both and
neither nor